Architecture in Conservation

One of the problems faced by museums and heritage organisations is adapting old buildings to their needs, or building new ones to fit in with historic sites. How exactly do you create a visitors' centre? How can a building be altered to accommodate a museum? The real difficulty lies where the budget is minimal and the potential damage to the environment or setting enormous.

Architecture in Conservation looks at the need to respond sensitively to the limitations or potentials of the environment. James Strike explains the strategies for producing new development at historic sites, examining the philosophy of conservation practice and stressing the importance of taking into account the characteristics of each individual site. He explains the way in which the methods of producing good developments relate to our very perception of history, and addresses the practical problems involved in developing appropriate sites. Case studies from around the world demonstrate the potential of each approach.

James Strike draws on his broad experience in architectural practice to show that a sensitive approach to these issues can unlock conservation problems and open up new opportunities for architectural expansion. *Architecture in Conservation* will be of considerable interest to site owners and architects responsible for site development, and to students of architecture and history.

James Strike was involved with design and new developments at English Heritage until 1993. He has now joined the team of conservation specialists in the Department of Conservation Sciences at Bournemouth University. He is the author of *Construction into Design* (1991).

The Heritage: Care–Preservation–Management programme has been designed to serve the needs of the museum and heritage community worldwide. It publishes books and information services for professional museum and heritage workers, and for all the organisations that service the museum community.

Editor-in-chief: Andrew Wheatcroft

The Development of Costume
Naomi Tarrant

Forward Planning: *A handbook of business, corporate and development planning for museums and galleries*
Edited by Timothy Ambrose and Sue Runyard

Heritage Gardens: *Care, conservation and management*
Sheena Mackellar Goulty

Heritage and Tourism: *In the global village*
Priscilla Boniface and Peter J. Fowler

The Industrial Heritage: *Managing resources and uses*
Judith Alfrey and Tim Putnam

Museum Basics
Timothy Ambrose and Crispin Paine

Museum Security and Protection: *A handbook for cultural heritage institutions*
ICOM and ICMOS

Museums 2000: *Politics, people, professionals and profit*
Edited by Patrick J. Boylan

Museums and the Shaping of Knowledge
Eilean Hooper-Greenhill

Museums without Barriers: *A new deal for disabled people*
Fondation de France and ICOM

The Past in Contemporary Society: Then/Now
Peter J. Fowler

The Representation of the Past: *Museums and heritage in the post-modern world*
Kevin Walsh

Architecture in Conservation

Managing Development at Historic Sites

James Strike

London and New York

First published 1994
by Routledge
11 New Fetter Lane, London EC4P 4EE

Simultaneously published in the USA and Canada
by Routledge
29 West 35th Street, New York, NY 10001

Typeset in Sabon by Florencetype Ltd, Kewstoke, Avon
Printed and bound in Great Britain by Butler & Tanner Ltd,
London and Frome
Printed on acid free paper

British Library Cataloguing in Publication Data
A catalogue record for this book is available from the British Library

Library of Congress Cataloging in Publication Data
Applied for

ISBN 0-415-08130-0

Contents

Illustrations

Acknowledgements

This book began as a series of notes which I produced when working in the Central Architectural Practice of English Heritage. I was at that time preparing reports for our Inspectors which related to listed building and grant applications where the proposals seemed to be moving in the wrong direction. My reports were to identify the important aspects of the historic site and to recommend a strategy by which the applicant could achieve a suitable response to their requirements for change. It was important that I justified the observations made, that I identified and explained the design concepts involved. Thus, my thanks and acknowledgement to English Heritage for this valuable time in formulating my thoughts. The development of these concepts, and their testing against examples, selected from many countries, has been carried out as a personal and independent task.

I wish to express my thanks to those who have helped with the illustrations. I have made extensive efforts to credit the origins, the illustrators, and the photographers, and I hope that any omission will be considered sympathetically.

My thanks also to the companies, practices, and organisations that have contributed to the material, the criticism, and production of this book. These are credited within the text, but I take this opportunity to name the following, who, each in their own way, have helped to make this book possible: Cezary Bednarski, Graham Binns, Bernard Blauel, Roger Bloomfield, Brian Blowers, Lyn and Richard Bryant, Duncan Campbell, Guido Canali, David Capon, Martin Carey, Brian Carter, Martin Charles, Eduardo Chillida, Arthur Chown, Hugh Clamp, Henry Cleere, Sue Cunningham, David Ellis, Jane Fawcett, Rosalind Field, Roger FitzGerald, Dennis Gilbert, Peter Gordon-Smith, Pamela Griffin, Neil Hanson, Nicholas Hare, Katy Harris, Birkin Haward, Elspeth Henderson, Robin Kent, Peter Kirkham, David Latham, Richard Linzey, Sam Lloyd, Jorg Mutz, Manfredi Nicoletti, Brendan O'Neill, Ken Osborne, Keith Parker, Richard Portchmouth, Liz Pride, David Rosenburg, John Russel, Mike Russum, John Rutherford, Philip Sayer, Susan Scanlon, Roger Stephenson, the late James Stirling, Horst Stuven, Peter Sutton, Mark Swenarton, Nick Turzynski, Jesus Uriarte, Robert Venturi, John Waldron, Wilfred Wang, Tony Weller, William Whitfield, Jonathan Wood, Paul Woodfield, and Tom Zetek.

And a special thanks to my wife Sarah and my sons Thomas and Edward for their patience, encouragement and assistance.

James Strike, 1993

1

Introduction

1.1 The aim of the book

If there is one issue that is likely to stir up a debate, it is that new architecture can be built at historic sites; that new architecture can stand successfully cheek by jowl with historic buildings.

This book confronts the debate. It steps back from the emotive and polarised position so often represented as 'historicism versus modernism'; that is, 'venerable historical styles versus ugly and impractical glass boxes', or, seen from the other viewpoint, 'pastiche of the past versus a confident expression of our age'. The book seeks some form of rationale; it seeks common ground, moving, not towards dogmatic statements of right or wrong, nor even towards a set of specific rules, but to tease out conceptual ideas which can be tested through actual examples to provide a clearer understanding of the problems and solutions. The aim is to provide an awareness of the issues, so that design decisions may be taken from a less emotive and more conscious viewpoint.

The subject matter is, therefore, both history and architecture. The hypothesis is that the design of new architecture for historic areas can be analysed, that design issues can be identified and used, not only to stimulate new design, but also as a tool in the evaluation and criticism of proposed schemes and completed projects.

1.2 Identifying the problem

Historic areas are progressively coming under threat of new development, not only in conservation areas but also at historic houses, gardens, and archaeological sites. The impact of new building work is noticed, not only at nationally important sites, but also in small conservation areas and remote archaeological humps and bumps in the countryside. History now has a high profile in people's lives. Section 2.2 'Present attitudes' covers a profile of current opinions; suffice it to say here that the increase of interest in history has led to a growth in the number of visitors to these areas. This in itself has raised the need for new buildings, but the pressure is compounded by other factors: we now have more leisure time and visitors expect to find better facilities at the sites; we have higher expectations for comfort, interpretation, education, cafés, and retail outlets. All of this has made historic areas a commercial commodity. Financiers realise the potential of investment in history, not only through visitor numbers and retail profits, but also through an increase in rent returns for commercial developments located amongst attractive old buildings and historic alleyways.

Building work is also needed in historic areas to protect the existing fabric of the sites and monuments. An array of techniques is available to consolidate and protect the old and fragile fabric (see section 7.3, 'Preservation or restoration'). However, such consolidation is not always practical, and a new protective building or a form of permanent cover may be necessary.

Finance, of course, plays an important part in the decision-making process (see section 8.2, 'Market forces'). This is an important element in the number of historic buildings which are 'at risk' through neglect. A survey by English Heritage[1] identified that some 7.3 per cent of historic buildings are at risk, and that these may be lost, and with them much of England's familiar historic townscape. Some of these buildings could be saved by the use of new building work. It is necessary to recognise the opportunities that could be opened up for a more economic use, or a change of use, through additional accommodation sensitively built alongside the existing buildings. This approach requires, amongst other things, a clear understanding of the design criteria involved. An awareness of design parameters allows for lateral thinking to unlock such schemes.

We need a method of controlling the pressure of new buildings at historic areas. We have in Great Britain one of the oldest and most developed systems of statutory planning control, and there are similar, yet interestingly different, systems in most other countries. There are also advisory bodies and preservation societies which work at both regional and international levels (see section 2.4, 'Guides and regulations'). These systems of influence have specific characteristics, that is, they are concerned predominantly with categories of use, volumetric size, and preservation of the status quo; they tend to pull back from aesthetics and the philosophy of conservation. Those who work in such bodies as English Heritage have a great wealth of historical knowledge and considerable experience in those technical and craft skills needed for repairs; what has been missing is the debate on the aesthetics of conservation. It is only recently that the role of new architecture has been considered as a possible option for conserving our past.

We now hear such phrases as 'architecture must be sympathetic to its surroundings' or 'the need for a sensitive approach'. What do these phrases mean? What do the adjectives 'sympathetic' and 'sensitive' connote? There is surely more to these words than personal likes and dislikes.

Such expressions are frequently used in a generalist way, giving the impression that the design qualities referred to are instinctive, that they are innate, involuntary, produced from some sort of genetic inheritance. If this is so, then design decisions are taken subconsciously, without forethought or appraisal. Surely there is more to this: surely the ability to make good design decisions can be acquired, taught, learnt, stimulated, and improved? The process can be developed into part of our conscious and cognitive system.

The words 'sympathetic' and 'sensitive' are terms of reference; they refer to some form of connection being made between the new architecture and the existing historic site; they ask for this connection to be of a certain quality. These connections are created by the designer; it is the role of the designer to see the opportunities and to bring them to reality. What are the characteristics of such connections? What are the similarities being created between the new and the old? How are they realised? What are their physical forms, their built reality, their architectural details? Is it possible to classify these attributes?

This book confronts such questions. Each chapter focuses on a separate approach and uses examples to illustrate the specific concept. The aim is to set up a framework, a media for design decisions taken clearly and consciously, a catalyst for informed debate.

1.3 The conservation field

The theme of the book, 'new architecture for conservation projects', needs to be seen as part of the whole field of conservation studies. It is a wide subject. If, however, it is seen to be divided into 'technical' aspects (mortar mixes, timber treatment, structural stability, etc.) and 'philosophical' aspects (selling history, archaeological excavations through layers of history, speculative reconstruction, etc.), then this book relates more to the latter.

It is only in the last thirty years that the 'philosophical' aspects of preservation have entered into the conservation debate. The debate is an on-going process which is now leading us to recognise that the philosophical aspects form an important part of the decisions that have to be made in the field of conservation. Issues such as the marketing of history, the control of visitor numbers, recognition of the special characteristics of each site, whether to preserve as found or restore to a specific period, all these need to be grasped and resolved for each site before any of the technical decisions can be taken. The physical questions – Should the ivy be stripped from the masonry walls? Should the nineteenth-century timber floor to be taken out of a medieval hall? Should the friable stone detail be treated with an alkoxysilane consolidant[2] or capped with a lead apron? – all depend on the overall philosophical strategy adopted for the specific site.

There are numerous books and articles on the technical aspects of conservation, and an excellent starting point for those unfamiliar with the subject would be *Conservation of Historic Buildings* by Sir Bernard Feilden (Feilden 1982).[3] Relatively few books have been published on the wider aspect of conservation and these are referred to in the text. However, it is useful to refer here to certain of these key texts to identify the conservation scene for this book.

First, the *ICOMOS Charter of 1966*.[4] ICOMOS (the International Council on

Monuments and Sites), is the principal organisation dealing with conservation on a worldwide basis. Representatives from many countries met in Venice in 1964 to set down 'the principles guiding the preservation and restoration of ancient buildings'.[5] These principles became the 1966 Charter. Several of the Articles form a useful base for the ideas explored in this book:

Article 1   The concept of an historic monument embraces not only the single architectural work but also the urban or rural setting in which is found the evidence of a particular civilisation, a significant development or an historic event . . .

Article 3   The intention in conserving and restoring monuments is to safeguard them no less as works of art than historical evidence.

Article 9   The process of restoration is a highly specialised operation. Its aim is to preserve and reveal the aesthetic and historic value of the monument and is based on respect for the original material and authentic documents. It must stop at the point where conjecture begins, and in this case, moreover, any extra work which is indispensable must be distinct from the architectural composition and must bear a contemporary stamp . . .

Article 12 Replacements of missing parts must integrate harmoniously with the whole, but at the same time, must be distinguishable from the original so that restoration does not falsify the artistic or historic evidence.

Article 13 Additions cannot be allowed except in so far as they do not detract from the interesting parts of the building, its traditional setting, the balance of its composition, and its relation with its surroundings.

The second publication, *Conservation Today*, was written by David Pearce[6] to accompany an exhibition at the Royal Academy in 1989 (Pearce 1989). Pearce argues that conservation should be a creative process and considers how legislation and finance can be used by public bodies, developers and amenity groups to stimulate attractive and sensitive schemes to save buildings at risk.

A third key text is *Re-Architecture, Old Buildings/New Uses*, written by Sherban Cantacuzino,[7] in which case studies show how the adaptation of redundant buildings, frequently incorporating the use of new architecture, can be handled with care and sensitivity (Cantacuzino 1989).

1.4 The scope of study

This book is concerned with the relationship between architecture and history. It is concerned with the role that architecture can play in preserving our heritage, and equally, it is concerned with the role that history can play in the generation of this new architecture needed to preserve our heritage. It is thus a two-way process, a symbiotic relationship between the new and the old.

What do we mean by 'new architecture'? For the purposes of this book there is no intention, or need, to provide a specific definition. However, in general terms, it considers cases where either additional accommodation is formed at the historic site, or where a new visual design statement is created amongst the existing fabric.

It considers this relationship between the new architecture and the existing fabric through an analysis of the design concepts involved. In doing so it acknowledges that this approach has to be seen in parallel with the pragmatic requirements of space, warmth, dryness, finance, and time. The art critic Umberto Eco, now known more for his historical novels, reminds us in *Art and Beauty in the Middle Ages* (Eco 1986) that the philosophy of aesthetics must not be allowed to become metaphysical but has to be related and tested through the reality of actual use.[8] Architecture for conservation has to be both functional and historically appropriate.

Finally, and confronting the paradox, the fact that the subject of this book is new architecture should not be construed as a wish to promote a bloom of new buildings at historic sites. On the contrary, all avenues have to be explored before action is taken. There will, however, be occasions where it is appropriate to introduce new architecture and the intention of this book is to stimulate an improvement of the quality of such architectural statements.

2

The field of study

We are dealing with a subject which is difficult to pin down, that is full of nuance and facets. Questions in conservation seem to change like the mood of light in the countryside; the facts and details may remain the same but our perspective, our interpretation, our light on the subject may well adjust. We are reminded of Claude Monet's thirty canvases of the west end of Rouen Cathedral; each covers the same subject, but each depicts a separate atmosphere, the light ranges from cool blues and greys to reflective white and burnt browns. As Monet wrote, 'tout change, quoique pierre'.[1]

The problem is that attitudes towards conservation vary, the pecking order of importance gets adjusted; adjusted over a period of time, and adjusted according to philosophical, political, and religious beliefs. Yet in spite of this, the subject still holds a solid core of identifiable aspects which can be studied. The art of architecture for conservation is not all subjective; much is objective, not necessarily in a modern quantifiable way, but nevertheless, assessable within specific criteria. The art historian E. H. Gombrich, in *Art and Illusion* (Gombrich 1960), clarifies how it is that the position of the observer related to a historical period may affect their point of view although the criteria available for making judgement remain the same.

We need to be able to recognise, and to justify, our position. Recognition of our own point of view is difficult enough, but to put these thoughts succinctly across to others requires a particularly clear understanding of the criteria. It is no longer acceptable to rely on outdated ideas of professionalism: 'I am a professional, therefore what I say is correct.' Obviously, the well-trained and experienced person will have a valuable contribution to make, but opinions now need to be explained, propositions have to be justified.

To do this we have to recognise not only the criteria of criticism, and these are explored in the following chapters, but also that conservation is not a static, deterministic commodity. We need to see our point of view as part of a maturing process, a reasoned response to change. This is needed to assist in the way we react to other people's points of view, and also to help us to cope with their adjustments to change.

It is necessary to consider these adjustments of attitude, not only to grasp a better perspective of our own opinions, but also to gain a clearer significance of the 'spirit of the age': that is, the idea that at any period of time there is a common belief. It was the philosopher Hegel who, in the early nineteenth century, proposed the idea of *Zeitgeist*, that is, that the *Geist*, or spirit, or 'mind' is manifested in everything at that particular time.[2] The proposition of a 'spirit of the times' indicates that this may vary from one time to another. Hegel refers to this change, this development, as 'the dialectical process' which he attributes to evolution of individual thought and the inherent conflicts that exist within individual issues.[3]

2.1 Views of history

Thus it is important to draw some form of perspective on the *Zeitgeist* of today. To arrive at this it is necessary to establish the evolution of events leading up to our present time: the spirit of the age needs to be seen not only as a single link in the chain of evolution, but also as a growth pattern where each period has an effect on the next. Each age may attempt to annihilate the opinions of its predecessors but, in spite of this, there is always some form of evolutionary influence. Opinions come round again after a period of time to form the growth pattern into a type of reiterative loop.

The following is a review of the evolution of attitudes towards conservation; it places particular emphasis on the ideas and opinions about the art of architecture within the field of conservation. It must be stressed that the study of conservation as a specific discipline is a relatively new subject; its origins stem from the birth of history as a separate subject, whence came the study of architectural and social history. The following observations are listed chronologically to trace this process of change.

It was common practice during the early centuries for building materials, especially stone, to be salvaged from disused buildings and redundant fortifications to construct new projects. The Anglo-Saxons and the Norman invaders made good use of the Roman sites as sources of building materials: where, for example, are the stones taken from London's Roman wall?[4] This is not to say that there was no duty of care by monarch or Church, but that the concern at that time was not to conserve buildings as a means of preserving history, but to conserve and embellish them as symbols of wealth, or to sanctify and glorify places of religious importance. Examples of deliberate demolition are commonplace, the destruction went on for centuries. What happened to the home of the Lancastrian monarchs at Richmond, Surrey?[5] Or to the fine ashlar taken as late as the 1830s from the buildings of the Blackfriars in Gloucester.[6]

Examples of new architecture constructed at historic sites during the medieval period are plentiful. The evidence is seen primarily in our cathedrals and large fortified houses. At Winchester in the fourteenth century, for example, Bishops Edington and William of Wykeham completely modernised the nave: the Norman structure was remodelled into the contemporary style of late Gothic.[7]

And at Gloucester Cathedral, a delicate and tenuous perpendicular Lady Chapel was built, uncompromisingly, up to the solid Norman east end.[8]

The dissolution of the monasteries between 1535 and 1539 contributed, unwittingly, to the germination of architectural conservation. The closure of 850 monastic houses engendered a feeling of loss, and thus a wish to restore, or at least to record, the past. (It also provided the sites which were to stimulate the interest in picturesque ruins during the eighteenth century.)

The conservation lobby was further strengthened by destruction of valuable buildings during Cromwell's Commonwealth of the 1650s. The Puritans sent their Commissioners on a punitive removal of religious images and 'superstitious' decorations from important churches and houses.

Little was written on the history of buildings prior to the seventeenth century. One of the earliest architectural texts to take a historical view about buildings of a previous age was Sir William Dugdale's *The History of St Paul's Cathedral in London from its Foundation until these Times*, 1658.[9]

The buildings of the Renaissance period created a number of architectural clashes with the new fashionable classical designs placed alongside, and even in front of, the embedded Gothic. Whatever discussion took place about the pros and cons of this new juxtaposition of new and old, the examples are so numerous that it must be assumed that there was little in the way of opposition or control against it. Inigo Jones's Banqueting Hall (1619–22) for example, must have been seen as aggressively modern and dominating against the rambling collection of its surrounding medieval structures;[10] and there is an assuredness in his new classical Renaissance portico for the west end of the old Gothic St Paul's Cathedral (1633–5) (see Fig. 2.1).[11]

History was not as sacrosanct in the seventeenth century as it is today. A false ceiling was installed beneath the Gothic vaults of St Stephen's Chapel in the Palace of Westminster to accommodate the Houses of Parliament, and in 1706 Sir Christopher Wren added oak panelling to the converted chapel which concealed the faded frescoes of the saints.[12]

The historian David Watkin,[13] in *The Rise of Architectural History* (Watkin 1980), points out that the history of art and architecture first became an academic discipline in Germany in the eighteenth century. This was long before similar developments in any other country in Europe. Notable publications include Fischer von Erlach, *A Plan of Civil and Historical Architecture, in the Representation of the Most Noted Buildings of Foreign Nations, both Ancient and Modern*, 1721, (translated into English 1730), and the influential text by J. J. Winckelmann *The History of Ancient Art*, 1764, (published in Boston 1880).[14]

The Society of Antiquaries of London received their royal charter in 1751. This group of eminent and learned persons (which had been in existence since the 1580s) established a reputation as the custodian of ancient monuments and as a pressure group to prevent the demolition of medieval remains.[15]

Figure 2.1. Old St Paul's Cathedral, London. Inigo Jones's classical portico added confidently to the front of the Gothic structure. (reproduced from Jane Fawcett, *The Future of the Past*)

By the mid-eighteenth century, views about the past had moved towards the 'picturesque', that is, an enjoyment of history based not on a sense of reason or research, but on the impact of the 'picture image' on the eye; a visual and immediate stimulant.[16] These views had been nurtured through the paintings of such artists as Claude Lorraine and Salvator Rosa, and influenced by the aesthetic writing of Edmund Burke, whose text of 1757, *A Philosophical Enquiry into the Origin of our Ideas of the Sublime and Beautiful*, proposed the idea that views seen by the eye were communicated not with the conscious mind, but through subconscious instincts, thus 'begetting passions'.[17] This passion was for 'nature'. M. W. Thompson in *Ruins, Their Preservation and Display*, sums this up:

> Religious attitudes towards ruins were greatly eased by the intrusion of the eighteenth-century belief in nature; giving God a place off-stage as it were. There was, in the contemplation of nature, a solace to be derived from a ruin.[18]

The impact of this eighteenth-century view of the past is seen through prints and paintings of the period. Contemporary drawings show an emotive idea of nature represented by untamed ivy and overgrown ruins shrouded in mystery and moonlight. A watercolour painted by James Lambert in 1785, of Bayham Abbey, Sussex, shows how contrived was the romance: the overgrown ruins of the Abbey were created by selective removal and buttressing to form a picturesque prospect from the house built on the far side of the lake.[19] It is clear that there was no desire for conservation as we know it today. The aim was not to preserve the past, but to use it as a theatrical effect to excite the visitor. The Rev. William Gilpin, travelling in 1770, observed of Tintern Abbey:

> Though the parts are beautiful, the whole is ill-shaped. No ruins of the tower are left, which might give form and contrast to the walls and buttresses, and other inferior parts. Instead of this, a number of gable-ends hurt the eye with their regularity, and disgust it by the vulgarity of their shape. A mallet judiciously used (but who durst use it?) might be of service in fracturing some of them.[20]

The second half of the eighteenth century seems strange in retrospect: it looked both back into history and forwards to the future. It looked backwards through the Gothic revival, where, for example, Horace Walpole developed Strawberry Hill with a desire for the monastic 'in memory of Eloisa's cloister', a tower which 'erects its battlements bravely', a 'little parlour' based on the sixteenth-century tomb of Ruthall, Bishop of Durham, the staircase with panelling modelled on Prince Arthur's early sixteenth-century tomb in Winchester Cathedral, and balusters copied from the library of Rouen Cathedral.[21] It looked forward through a fascination in the scientific experiments which were moving more into the public domain.

By the beginning of the nineteenth century, the nature of criticism and imagination is represented by the 'Gothic novel'. There was a strange interweaving of interests between the new sciences and the darkness of the past; a fascination with historicism and a fictitious fear of science epitomised by Mary Shelley's novel *Frankenstein* of 1816.[22]

More medieval architecture was lost during the Gothic revival by over-conjectural 'restoration' than by demolition. Jane Fawcett explores this in *The Future of the Past* (Fawcett 1976), and attributes the loss to over-zealousness and over-confidence. The Gothic style was seen as the correct architectural expression for devout religious conviction actively fostered through the zeal of the Oxford Movement[23] and the 'Ecclesiologists'.[24] This single-mindedness gave architects little regard for accuracy of the past; their aim was to correct the mistakes of their forefathers and to regularise all the decay, patina and muddle that had built up through the previous layers of history (see section 4.4, 'Layers of history'). Many interiors, numerous churches, and several of the cathedrals were 'restored' according to current ideology rather than historical research. Examples include the Norman west end tower of Canterbury Cathedral which was rebuilt in 1834 to match its Gothic twin; symmetry was gained at the expense of Lanfranc's robust tower. Similarly, the west end of St Alban's Abbey, which was completely remodelled by Lord Grimthorpe into the Gothic style between 1879 and 1895.[25]

There was a reaction against this conjectural restoration. Pugin visited Hereford Cathedral in 1833 and was horrified at Wyatt's 'vile and rascally work' to the west end, and by the 'Saxon ornaments imitated in plaster in the most wretched style, a plain ceiling in the nave, and the Lady Chapel filled with bookcases with the end towards the church plastered up'.[26] Ruskin was equally single-minded in his criticism of alterations around the country.

In 1877 William Morris founded the Society for the Protection of Ancient Buildings. Its *Manifesto* indicates the nature of their criticism:

> [ancient buildings] have become the subject of one of the most interesting of studies, and of an enthusiasm, religious, historical, artistic, which is one of the undoubted gains of our time; yet we think that if the present treatment of them be continued, our descendants will find them useless for study and chilling to enthusiasm.

Morris goes on to say that any restoration which has to be made should be:

> wrought in the unmistakable fashion of the time. . . . The results [being] a building in which the many changes, though harsh and visible enough, were, by their very contrast, interesting and instructive and could by no possibility mislead.

The text portrays a rosy view of history in the wish to preserve the 'living spirit' and 'the appearance of antiquity' in the 'partly-perished work of the ancient craftsmaster'. The idea of cleaning the whole building would have been resisted:

> the whole surface of the building is necessarily tampered with . . . the reckless stripping of buildings . . . [the surface] made neat and smooth by the tricky hand of some unoriginal and thoughtless hack of today.

11

The Victorian 'spirit of the age' was steeped in the past. They considered 'the past' to be worthy, and a suitable model for the present. They saw the various historical styles as representing chivalry, honour, or rectitude.[27] There was rivalry between the styles: Gothic revival, Greek revival, and later all sorts of historical and colonial interests such as Egyptian and Indian revivals. The intense competition to design the new buildings for Downing College, Cambridge reads, in Cinza Sicca's *Committed to Classicism* (Sicca 1987), like an Anthony Trollope novel. There were collegiate rows and parliamentary questions before William Wilkins's Greek revival scheme was selected.

The Ancient Monuments Protection Act came into force in Britain in 1882. This was the first time the government had taken a positive role in the protection of historic sites, albeit rather tentatively due to the lobby of protest against interference with private property. The Act scheduled as few as sixty-eight prehistoric earthworks, burial mounds, and stone circles. Little did they realise that this would lead within a hundred years to the present schedule of 13,000 ancient monuments and the listing of 440,000 historic buildings. (For those unfamiliar with the system in Britain, ancient monuments are *scheduled* and historic buildings are *listed* under separate Acts.)

By the end of the century, the ancient monuments of most of Europe were covered by protective legislation of varying degrees of authority, and the USA enacted its first Federal Antiquities Law in 1906.[28]

The First World War (1914–18) upset the social balance. It took away many young men, servants became scarce, and the class structures were eroded. The days of the serviced country estate were over and the rich industrialists gave up building historic, look-alike country houses: this is the time of Isabel Colegate's novel *The Shooting Party* (Colegate 1980). Emancipation[29] eroded the upper classes' privileged enjoyment of history and the lower class became less a victim of their past.

Care of the government stock of archaeological sites, historic buildings, and medieval ruins in England was carried out by the Office of Public Buildings and Works. Their approach during the interwar period was one of tidiness and straight lines. Preservation consisted of taking out the undergrowth and the ivy, removing loose stones, repointing and capping the walls, and providing close-cut grass with neat edges. The guide books were of a standard academic format full of historical detail.

It was not until 1932 that any protection was given to historic buildings in Britain through the first of the Town and Country Planning Acts.

Buildings of the Modern Movement first appeared in Germany at the beginning of the nineteenth century: albeit, the roots of the movement had begun earlier in England through the Industrial Revolution and the industrial mills, and through experiments in concrete in both England and France.[30] Buildings of the Modern Movement arrived in Britain and the USA during the 1920s and 1930s: they set out to be totally non-historical and as such they were seen as a threat to history.

The Second World War (1939–45) shattered the historic core of many cities – Warsaw, Berlin, Dresden, and in Britain, Coventry and Portsmouth. Thousands of historic buildings were destroyed or damaged. Limited resources at the end of the war went to survival and economic recovery; restoration and conservation were low priorities. Requirements of the war effort also moved construction techniques further into industrialisation and this was used after 1945 for mass housing such as the prefab scheme[31] and later for tower blocks.[32] The spirit of the age after the war was for a better future based on industrial progress. Social beliefs and aesthetic judgements were based on a need for space, health, and education, rather than on cultural heritage. The early industrial mills, for example, which we now regard as heritage buildings, were considered as an architectural legacy of worn-out and inefficient production and as places of social exploitation.

Restoration of one particular building after the war needs to be looked at in detail as it represents one of the earliest uses of modern design for a conservation project. The Alt Pinakothek in Munich, 1826–36, was designed by Leo von Klenze as part of Ludwig I of Bavaria's dream to turn Munich into the Venice of the North. The centre of this long neo-classical building was torn open by a bomb during the war and something had to be done so that the priceless contents could be returned from their safe-keeping in the countryside. The architect Hans Döllgast saw this as an opportunity to test the philosophy of the Modern Movement. He had trained under Peter Behrens, one of the founders of the movement, and had been appointed as Professor at the Munich Technische Hochschule just before the war.[33] His scheme, prepared in 1952, for the restoration of the Pinakothek was not only modern but also managed to reflect the rhythm and basic shapes of the original building (see Fig. 2.2). The slender 250mm steel columns which were used to replace the 19-metre high brick piers destroyed from the elevation made use of the latest technology developed in the munitions factories. The new sections of roof were formed in the new building material of aluminium. Döllgast inserted two straight staircases into the missing parts of the south loggia to form improved circulation around the museum. Although his scheme to enclose these with a modern glass wall was later rejected in favour of brick, the foyer space today still has a powerful and modern feel. Bernhard Blauel gives a full account of the story in *Hans Döllgast 1891–1974*.[34] He refers to Döllgast's conviction that 'the building had a history, and the scar from the bomb was part of that history; to hide it seemed absurd' (see section 4.4, 'Layers of history'). Blauel comments that the scheme represents one of the first examples of the bold yet sensitive approach similar to that now used by Carlo Scarpa at Castelvecchio, Verona,[35] and by Foster at the Royal Academy, London (see Fig. 8.3). It must be pointed out that Döllgast was able to convince the authorities on the grounds of cost and time, and that although his approach was common to the ethos of the Modern Movement, it had not yet become part of the *Zeitgeist*. His work was a lonely example; such is the nature of change.

Returning now to the chronological listing, many areas of close-knit terrace houses were demolished in the 1960s under the name of slum clearance, particularly in those historic cities that expanded out of the Industrial

13

Revolution. There were, of course, dwellings which were beyond restoration or unsuitable for upgrading to a reasonable standard of facilities. None the less, the rules of classification for a slum became progressively more rigorous as the spirit of industrialisation demanded more sites to be cleared for concrete town centres and rows of tower blocks.

The thrust for the future was influenced during the 1960s by a push for material gain. Architecture and planning were fuelled by profit. Decisions were justified and veiled behind social progress and aims for a better future; history got in the way of progress and 1968 saw the demolition of the greatest number of listed buildings recorded in one year.

English Heritage was set up under the 1983 National Heritage Act. This brought together various government departments that had been dealing with conservation. Lord Montagu of Beaulieu, its first Chairman, recalls that historic monuments were at that time still:

> forbidding places for the visitor. They were indeed well cared for, but the visitor faced a rather daunting custodian dressed like a prison warder, complete with jangling keys, whose main job seemed to be to tell them to keep off the grass.[36]

In 1988 the 'thirty-year rule' was adopted in England by which modern buildings thirty years old could be protected under the Planning Acts. Eighteen buildings, including the Royal Festival Hall[37] and the large concrete spans of Stockwell Bus Garage,[38] were covered.

This then is the history which leads us up to today's attitudes. It is salutary to see current conservation practice as part of this continuous process of change.

2.2 Present attitudes

What is the 'the spirit of the age' in the 1990s? There is certainly a common reaction against the strident tower blocks and the mean, curtain-walled offices seen in so many urban areas. These are perceived as the products of 'modern architecture' and the reaction against them has led to the present wish for 'historical-looking' buildings. Two observations need to be made about this attitude. First, it associates modern architecture with that produced in the materialistic 1960s and fails to recognise that modern design has moved a long way forward since then. Second, a society that looks backwards with blinkered eyes is unable to express any sense of optimism for the present age, let alone for the future.

The present wish for an architecture that is retrospective is seen in the drawn-out debate on the design for redevelopment of the Paternoster site at St Paul's Cathedral, London. The proposals from the 1987 competition upset a lot of people who wanted a more 'historical' solution. The *Evening Standard*, who sponsored John Simpson's neo-classical planning application, carried out a Gallup survey of visitors to the exhibition of the schemes.[39] The outcome was

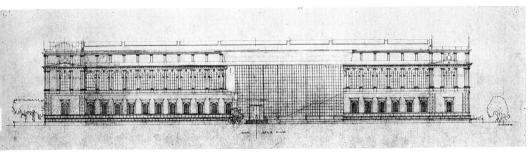

Figure 2.2. Alt Pinakothek, Munich. Hans Döllgast's restoration after the Second World War; an early example of the use of modern design in conservation. (a) New steel columns used to replace the brick piers. (b) Unrealised scheme to enclose the damaged elevation within a modern glass wall. (Architektur Museum Technischen, Universität München)

clear-cut in that three out of four wanted classical-style buildings (see section 7.5, 'Building history').

Public interest in the past is also seen in the growth of 'living history' projects. This has been big business in America for several decades, particularly at Williamsburg where several buildings (including the seventeenth-century Governor's House and the nineteenth-century hospital) have been completely rebuilt and occupied with actors in period costume. The first in England was the Jorvik Viking Centre, where visitors are transported through a reconstructed village with animation, noise, and smells. This was followed with similar presentations of Chaucer's *Canterbury Tales*, Oxford's *Life at the University*, and Tunbridge Wells's *A Georgian Journey*. History is a commodity: you are even invited to visit the catacombs of Kensal Cemetery in north London.

There is a danger that this type of contact with history may be superficial. Anthony Smith, President of Magdalen College, Oxford, regrets that the university is falling victim to an unthinking tourist culture: 'I object to the way that people are invited to consume institutions such as Oxford rather than understand them'.[40] Julian Spalding, Director of Manchester City Art Gallery, also identified these conflicts of presentation in his paper to The Royal Society of Arts, entitled 'Art Galleries: Church or Funfair? Museums in a Democracy'.[41] Speaking against the galleries set up in the 1960s with grey walls and the pictures in a line, each set in its own space:

> The attack on the standard gallery came from two sides: those art historians who saw art within a social and political context, particularly the Structuralists and the Marxists, and those art historians who saw art within the context of the history of style.

And against the modern popularist approach:

> all physical sensations brought to play, all cares and the enquiring mind forgotten . . . that we should let the consumer choose, and indeed, be judged by the consumer's choice.

This *Zeitgeist* is for a popular demand for history, as a means of relaxation, history seen as an easy and immediate form of entertainment, as if it were detached from the reality of the past.

The opening scene of Peter Shaffer's stage play *Lettice and Lovage* is a group of downcast and bored tourists being shown round Fustian House, a gloomy sixteenth-century building. The guide points out the family motto above the staircase, '*Lapsu surgo*' – 'By a fall I rise'. A succession of visitors pass through the hall, and by the time the fourth group arrives the anecdote about the motto has grown from 'Her Majesty would have fallen had not her host taken hold of her arm', to 'You are looking at what is indisputably the most famous staircase in England. . . . The staircase of Aggrandizement. . . . The Virgin Queen Elizabeth was saved from almost certain death by a feat of daring, completely unachievable today.' There is a tendency to indulge in the past, to edit it and embroider it, to see its rosy side.

This demand for history is seen in the amount of public debate about architecture and in the growth of demand to save anything that is old. There is a sentiment for the past. The architectural critic Martin Pawley is concerned enough about this preservationist attitude to state that the infrastructure of our towns cannot survive; that the needs of towns are being forced by the conservation lobby into the supershed shopping centres and distribution points built in the countryside around the cities.[42]

Conservation is now an international concern, issues are international news. ICCROM (The International Centre for the Study of the Preservation and the Restoration of Cultural Property) was founded by UNESCO in 1959, and ICOMOS (The International Council on Monuments and Sites) set their Conservation Charter in 1966.

National preservation groups are also joining internationally, notably DOCOMOMO (The International Working Party for the Documentation and Conservation of Buildings, Sites and Neighbourhoods of the Modern Movement), which held its first international conference at Eindhoven in 1990.

It is interesting to observe that, in spite of this increase in international debate, there are still differences of emphasis within the various countries; national characteristics still influence conservation practice.

Central Europe has a strong commitment towards rebuilding history, the response to extensive destruction during the Second World War has been to replicate many of the lost national monuments and city centres. Compare, for example, the rebuilding of Dresden against the new town schemes for Coventry and Portsmouth.

Another variant is seen in France, where building important projects in the heart of historic areas is used as a political gesture. Successive Presidents have commissioned 'des grands projets', almost vying with one another: the Centre National d'Art et de Culture in Les Halles; the National Opera House facing on to Place de la Bastille; and the vast structure of the Arche de la Défense, placed proudly on the important historical axis from the Palais du Louvre, Champs-Elysées, and Arc de Triomphe.

Pursuing the political dimension. It is interesting to observe how the Georgian houses of Dublin are now seen more as part of the valuable Irish inheritance rather than a sign of their colonialist past: the elegant houses in such areas as Henrietta Street are being taken up by Dubliners and carefully restored. The Ministry of Works in Ireland is also benefiting from politics through grants from the European Commission to provide new facilities at some of their more important historical sites: at Dublin Castle, for example, where an international conference centre has been unobtrusively inserted, and in Phoenix Park, where a new interpretation centre has been placed with confidence alongside Ashtown Castle.

There is an air of confidence in Italy. Here, however, interest in new architecture at historic sites is about the spirit of modernity in design; they enjoy the aesthetic tension between modern detailing placed against historic fabric. Architects such as Carlo Scarpa at Castelvecchio (see section 4.4, 'Layers of history'), and Guido Canali at Palazzo della Pilotta (see Fig. 5.1) are willing, and permitted, to experiment. There is an immediacy and exuberance in their work. Italians accept this approach as commonplace; they have hosted the world-renowned Architectural Biennale in Venice since the epoch-making exhibition of 1981, 'The Presence of the Past'.

And finally, the reticence of the English. Nikolaus Pevsner in *The Englishness of English Art*[43] explores, through English architectural history, the English sense of detachment, distrust of the extreme, a wish for moderation and reasonableness, a holding back (Pevsner 1956, Chapter 3). The trio of famous English architects – Foster, Rogers, and Stirling – received acclaim for their work abroad before recognition at home. Stirling believes that distrust of modern design in Britain has 'set the cause of good architecture back in favour of a "Georgian" revival'.[44] His extension of the Tate Gallery, London, to form the Clore Gallery, met with a mixed reaction. For many it had a European edge to it: it was too stark, too blatant, too un-English.

2.3 The special character of historic sites

Why do we value historic sites? It is self-evident that they are old, but what is it about being old that gives them a value? Their primary importance is as a document of history, a source of information, a record, a primary source for research, evidence which can be experienced by each generation: they act as the 'what, why, and how' of our predecessors.

The abbreviation ICCROM (International Centre for the Study of the Preservation and the Restoration of Cultural Property) uses the description 'cultural' property. Culture is about a refined understanding of the arts and other intellectual achievements, it is about customs of a particular age.[45] This then ties culture down to the 'best' of an age, or the 'most representative' of an age; it removes the definitions about the importance of a site away from current fashion to a broader, long-term perspective. George Steiner[46] reminds us that our present culture has the benefit of the best periods of the past:

> The Greeks, the incomparable begetters of philosophy, cultivation of poetic and speculative speech.
> The Florentine Renaissance, the abiding model of aesthetic and political excellence.
> The Enlightenment, porticoes of our public edifices, the canonic source of beauty.
> And Modern imagination, ecstatic immediacy to the divine.[47]

Culture, in its widest sense, is an important characteristic of our historic sites.

The nature of historic buildings is also explored through the analytical work of Gill Chitty.[48] She identifies the process by which a property gradually transforms over the years from a new building to a ruin. Her paper, 'A prospect of ruins'[49] identifies the stages of decay in this life-cycle of a building:

stage 1
The building's architectural design and construction, probably over a period of time, and possibly on the site of an earlier building.

stage 2
Its useful life as a group of working buildings with all the alterations and additions that become necessary with changes in taste and use.

stage 3
The abandonment of the building for occupation or other functions. On monastic sites there is often an immediate period of demolition and robbing; in the case of a domestic or defensive building this event might take the form of fire, siege or obsolescence, and a deliberate slighting.

stage 4
The building is now a 'ruin'. A period follows during which the ruins are derelict and the processes of decay advance dilapidation, possibly accompanied by further salvage of building materials and casual use for agriculture or other purposes.

stage 5
A period when the visual or 'picturesque' value of the ruins is recognised. Some tampering may take place to enhance the visual effect. This period in the eighteenth or nineteenth centuries includes the deliberate creation of ruins from historic fabric.

stage 6
A period when the historical, as well as the visual, value of the ruin as a monument is recognised and attempts are made to arrest the process of decay and to protect the remains. Records, historical research and accurate drawings are undertaken.

stage 7
Finally preservation: a period when attempts are made to stabilise the structure, to reinstate the ruin following investigation, possibly including the reassembly of fallen masonry, or even reconstruction with new material.

Chitty's classification helps to identify the nature of what we are preserving, and as such, how to deal with it. It is a means of answering questions. It would, for example, be reasonable to put in a replica sash window in stage 1; a suitably designed modern window in stage 2; and to let the ivy grow in stage 4. The clarification is useful for the designer of new architecture needed for the site; it is useful to have a clear idea about the site you are working on.

Methods have been attempted to set up a system of analysis of the architectural quality of historic sites. These were particularly popular as a product of the determinist approach of the 1950s and 1960s. One of the more successful schemes was that set up by Professor Cordingly at the School of Architecture of the University of Manchester.[50] This, using a matrix of standard observations, was able to classify the physical properties of the building (size, type, materials, etc.) but was less adaptable to capture the cultural and aesthetic qualities of the site.

Reference must be made to David Lowenthal's book *The Past is a Foreign Country*; this explores the 'benefits and burdens of the past' (Lowenthal 1985, Chapter 2). He covers history in a wider scope than just architectural sites, nevertheless, his observations highlight the psychological traits by which we assess historical sites. He considers the benefits of history under the following headings: *familiarity*, we can perceive only what we are accustomed to, objects that lack any familiar elements or configurations remain incomprehensible; *validation*, historical precedent legitimates what exists today; *identity*, the sureness of 'I was' is a necessary component of the sureness of 'I am'; *guidance*, study of the past might enable men to foretell the future; *enrichment*; and *escape*. Lowenthal also identifies the 'valued attributes' of history, including: *precedence*, *remoteness*, *primordial*, and *continuity*.

2.4 Guides and regulations

It is convenient to group existing guides and regulations into three categories: legislative documents, design guides, and related reading.

The historical background to legislative documents related to conservation was mentioned in section 2.1, 'Views of history'. It is not my intention to work systematically through the legal procedures, but some key phrases within the current documents do help to shed light on our present design philosophy. The National Heritage Act for England refers to the requirement not only to preserve ancient monuments and historic buildings but also 'to promote the enhancement of the character and appearance of conservation areas'.[51] The implication being that the status quo is no longer satisfactory and that the government is looking for any change to represent an improvement. The Act also makes requirement 'to promote the public's enjoyment of, and advance their knowledge of, ancient monuments and historic buildings'.[52] Any change must, therefore, not only improve the situation, but also move towards a more approachable presentation. Similar phrases occur in other documents to underline the importance of improvement and a higher standard of design. It is interesting to follow specific cases through the law courts to see how the interpretation of such words as 'enhancement' is challenged and defined. The British government has talked about moving further into the control of visual matters through design guides: in 1990 Mr Patten, then Minister for the Environment, speaking at the Royal Fine Arts Commission, outlined the need for government codes which 'would point the way in matters of scale, layout, public open space, and context'.[53]

The most common form of design guide is that produced by regional and local planning departments. There are many versions of these generalist pamphlets covering the sort of problems that occur throughout the country: domestic extensions, windows, shop fronts, etc. These vary in quality and it would be better if greater use were made of national publications. In America, for example, these common design problems are covered in one document produced by the Secretary of the Interior for the National Parks Service. This, the *Guidelines for Rehabilitating Historic Buildings*, is a sensible list of do's and don'ts to control materials, replacement of historic features, roofs, windows, store fronts, fixtures, and landscape.

Of equal interest are the guides that relate to particular regional or local design problems. These range from the specific detailing of roofing tiles in Hampstead Garden Suburb, or patterned brickwork in Reading, to design guides for large areas of towns where it is important to retain the coherent nature of the existing buildings and spaces, for example, in the Regency town of Leamington Spa, or to co-ordinate visual improvements along Pennsylvania Avenue, Washington, DC.

Related specifically to new building work at historic sites are the new procedures for archaeological investigation. The proposals, instigated by the City of York, introduce advisory guidelines to assist the development of sites where there is an archaeological interest. The proposal being that development within designated areas will be preceded by archaeological evaluation covered by a fee from the developer. Destruction of less than 5 per cent of the archaeological remains will be regarded as an acceptable compromise.

We tend to underestimate the importance of related reading. It is better to have a well-informed team, including the client, rather than a tight system of control. Related reading includes all of those books that refer to architecture at historic sites within the framework of a wider, or different subject. The bibliography at the end of this book lists many of these, and several other articles are named in the text. The design process is seldom straightforward and it is often necessary to focus for a while on one of the related subjects. The designer may, for example, need to clarify an idea about external space between the new and the old through reference to Cliff Moughtin, *Urban Design, Street and Square* (Moughtin 1992), or more specific research through an understanding of the particular qualities of a specific architect, or the options for altering a church interior guided and informed through study of Andrew Freeman, *English Organ Cases* (Freeman 1921).

All of these texts help to broaden our perspective on the factors to be considered when designing within a historical context. It is important to see these not as restrictions, but as factors to be taken on board and used to advantage. The designer must remain independent yet willing to justify the proposals. Hopefully, the following chapters will help with this.

3

Connections by association

Chapter 1 identified the need to establish some sort of sympathetic connection between the new architecture and the historic site. Chapter 2 set the scene within the field of conservation studies. This chapter considers how this relationship can be formed by use of 'association'. The concept is simple, but the realisation is complicated: it is complicated by both the subtlety and the evasiveness of the subject.

Regrettably, it is necessary to tackle this complexity at an early stage in the book as the ideas involved underlie the development of the following chapters. This chapter is, of necessity, rather philosophical but rest assured that the remaining chapters become more straightforward and related to real examples.

3.1 The concept of association

The concept, in its simplest form, is that a new piece of architecture can be designed to remind the observer of another building. The observer recognises the similarities between the new architecture and that other building and thus bestows these same characteristics on to the new architecture. It is up to the designer, when working at a historic site, to stimulate this connection with another building which has the qualitative characteristics similar to those of the historic site.

A straightforward example is Michael Hopkins's Mound Stand at Lord's Cricket Ground, London (Fig. 3.1). The shape and material of the roof evoke an image of a row of marquee tents. The observer is reminded of summer days, Edwardian parties, county cricket, and cucumber sandwiches. The new stand is thus bestowed with the characteristics inherent in the site, it becomes conjoined with the 'spirit of cricket'. The new architecture can be seen as an abstract of the characteristics of the site. Hopkins avoids the conventional cantilevered engineering solution in favour of an image more appropriate to the site.

3.2 The role of perception

Unfortunately, the phenomenon is not usually as straightforward as this, and it

Figure 3.1. The Mound Stand, Lord's Cricket Ground, London. Michael Hopkins. Canvas roofs which evoke an association with marquee tents and summer days. (photograph Martin Charles)

is necessary to take some careful steps forward to appreciate the subtleties of the concept.

The idea of forming an association between a piece of new architecture and a historic site relies on the way the observer perceives the new architecture. It relies on how the observer perceives the *references* in the new architecture; how the observer perceives these references in terms of that other building; and how the observer perceives the references in association with the historic site. Perception plays an important role in this process; that is, how we understand the building, how we see it, our views about it.

It would be useful to look at some basic principles about perception.[1] We receive sensations through our sense organs of sight, hearing, touch, and smell. We respond to these stimuli, either as a reflex action, 'I jump when I stand on a sharp object' (an action which is without conscious thought); or as a cognitive action, 'I consider the alternatives and therefore respond thus' (an action based on conscious thought).

Perception is the act of interpreting the information that we receive via our sense organs. We receive the data, assess them, and formulate a point of view. Take the analogy in the comparison between a photograph of a landscape, and a painting of the same scene. The photograph makes an exact record of the scene, but the painting depicts the scene as perceived by the artist. The eye receives data, the mind perceives them. We receive the data into our mind and we consider them in relationship to our previously acquired knowledge; we ascertain their values in comparison with our past experiences, we perceive their significance.

It is through the process of perception that we are able to form connections between things. We perceive the similarity between objects, and between abstract ideas; we are even able to perceive connections between objects and abstract ideas. It is this ability to make perceptual connections which forms the basis of the architectural concept of association.

Looking at a building is, therefore, more than receiving its image on the retina; it is to do with how we interpret this information against our bank of previous knowledge and experience. Our appreciation of the building is, therefore, more than what it looks like on the outside, our previous experience leads us on to opinions as to its internal organisation, its possible use, and its position in history.[2]

3.3 Cognitive and instinctive actions

It is necessary to look carefully at the process of forming associations. There is a danger in the simplified classification of actions as being either reflex or cognitive; in reality the border is blurred. It is blurred owing to our tendency to transfer some of our conscious actions into a subconscious state. For example, what may begin as a conscious action may, if frequently repeated, become a habit: we perform these habitual actions instinctively: 'I was taught how to tie my shoe laces, I use this information every morning, I now do it instinctively.'

It is necessary to broaden the classification of types of action. At one end of the spectrum are the reflex actions, at the other end, the cognitive actions, and, in the centre, the instinctive actions. We are born with innate reflex actions, we think through and calculate cognitive actions, and we subconsciously recall previous knowledge and experiences for our instinctive actions.

Our use of perception to recognise factual or abstract similarities between things – that is to form associations – can operate at either the cognitive level or the instinctive level. It is often difficult to recognise which is being used: we seldom stop to ask ourselves, 'Was that an instinctive or a cognitive action?' It is, however, important to recognise that many of our judgements involve a degree of instinctive intuition.

The significance of these ideas needs to be seen through actual examples. What thoughts do we have about particular buildings? What feelings do they evoke? What memories are stimulated? What associations made?

3.4 Buildings as symbols

The simplest starting point is the idea of a building as a symbol. Big Ben is seen as a symbol of London, an icon of Parliament in the capital city; similarly, the Eiffel Tower is a symbol of Paris: most large cities have their specific image. These symbols relate to a specific place. Other symbols relate to different issues. Different architectural features create different symbolic meanings: if we see a spire we assume it is a church; the sight of a crenellated parapet evokes the idea of a castle; a group of brick stacks reminds us of industrial buildings. The cluster of brick chimneys which once stood in Burnley, Lancashire, for example, must have been a clear image of the town's industrial base. Regrettably, many of these chimneys were demolished in the 1960s, but fortunately, the area has now been designated a conservation area[3] and the remaining stacks saved. These symbols act as a trigger for our perceptive recall, we are reminded of an actual place, or building, or type of building.

The architectural symbol can also suggest a particular characteristic, an abstract idea or emotion: the portcullis as a symbol of strength and defence; the Regency bow window is associated with genteel life and refinement; the Norfolk latch as a symbol of rural dwelling. We have to recognise, however, that the common understanding of a symbol can sometimes change. A particular event can boost, dent, or modify its meaning. We have to remind ourselves that the swastika was an ancient symbol of good luck – once used by Rudyard Kipling on the cover of all his books – long before it was hijacked by the Nazis.[4]

Symbols contribute to the way we understand a building, the way we read it. As words impart a message to the reader, so images have a vocabulary which can also be read. Words can be used to form useful associations: 'Indomitable',

'Thunderer', 'Formidable', and 'Centurion' have all been selected as names for the heavy diesel locomotives pulling out of Waterloo station;[5] the names set up an association with the power of the engines. Similarly, architectural images can be set up to be read.

It is interesting to observe that while illiteracy and innumeracy are now recognised as social handicaps, there is no such word to describe people who are visually unaware; we may describe these people as visually illiterate.

Peter Davey, in 'Museums and Memory',[6] clarifies that 'reading' architecture is not strictly a one-way process. Writing about the way we interact with a museum, he reflects:

> As we move around a gallery, we add our own perceptions and memories to the stories that we are told there and, in the same way as reading a novel, we engage in our imaginations with the author and the text.[7]

The author Marcel Proust has this ability to trigger a memory of the past through a recall of those unforeseen moments of illumination which flash vivid memories across our inner screen of vision.[8] Günter Grass's powerful novel *The Tin Drum* (Grass 1959) uses the process of Erick's prolonged and mesmeric beating of his tin drum to portray his attempt to drum up the past. Umberto Eco points out in *The Open Work* (Eco 1989) that any work of art (including architecture) contains an 'open end' in so far as the observer's response is subject to his or her own previous experiences rather than that of the designer.

Architecture can act as a symbol in many ways. The type of construction, its structural system, its details, and its materials all contribute to the way that it is read.[9] Solid stone construction evokes a sense of permanence; soft irregular brickwork is associated with hand-crafted rural skills; hard-edged regular brickwork with industry and precision; and white glazed brickwork with light wells and hygiene (see section 6.5, 'Syntax and detail'). The structure of a building can be designed to express structural forces associated with heavy engineering, or tensile members to express the images of a lightweight structure (see section 6.2, 'Morphology'). These are the words of architecture, the codes, the symbols, the plot, the story line.

It is these architectural symbols which can be used to manipulate the observer's attitude. The designer can incorporate such symbols into the new piece of architecture so that the observer, consciously or subconsciously, makes a connection between these symbolic aspects and the referential characteristic, mood, feeling, or memory, of the origins of the reference. The designer stimulates this association between the new architecture and the origins of the symbol. The skill comes in selecting an association that is appropriate to the historical significance of the specific location.

It must be pointed out that this process of relating new architecture to historic sites through the formation of association does not always succeed. A gesture which failed is the tier above tier of cantilevered concrete offices which rise over the Victorian shops in Bingley, designed to echo the nearby Five-Rise canal locks, but the scale and detailing do not trigger the desired response.[10]

The philosophical study of this subject makes use of the medical term 'semiotics', which is concerned with symptoms, derived from the Greek *semeiotikos* ('of signs'). This is the route taken by Umberto Eco in his analytical art appreciation; it is evident in his later novels.[11]

3.5 Ideas and emotions

So far it has been assumed that the connection between the new piece of architecture and the historic site is made via an association with another building; that is, via a characteristic from within the field of architecture. As this process involves using another building to generate an idea or emotion, then it would seem reasonable that the connection could equally be formed by using not another building, but another object, or even an abstract idea taken from outside the field of architecture. This is indeed the case.

A straightforward example is the Royal Saltworks at Arc-et-Senans. Ledoux creates a direct architectural reference to 'the flow of saline water' for the motifs on the elevations. Extending the connection to an abstract idea is seen during the 1930s through the interest in transport and speed taken up in architecture through the 'ocean liner' elements of sun decks and balcony rails at such buildings as the De la Warr Pavilion, Bexhill; and the explicit example of the 1938–9 Birmingham aerodrome with its large canopy wings cantilevered out each side as an overt reference to the aeroplanes of the period.

The idea that symbols can be used to express particular ideas was central to the work and writing of Robert Venturi in the 1960s. His influential book, *Complexity and Contradiction in Architecture* (Venturi 1966) was a reaction against the pragmatic and functional approach of the period; it searched for an architecture that was more than a response to the functional programme, an architecture which reflected the intricacy of both the pragmatic and the emotional realities of the project. He developed these ideas through his work and his later book *Learning from Las Vegas* (Venturi 1972).

The title *Complexity and Contradiction in Architecture*, indicates that the issues are both involved and evasive. Nevertheless, it is important to explore the complexities in order to appreciate the richness of the ideas. The subtleties of the subject centre around the nature by which the references are transferred. This is difficult to discuss in purely architectural terms, and it is necessary to make use of comparisons within other art forms. In doing so, it is recognised that such comparisons are not always totally appropriate. It is, however, in recognition of their differences that the nature of associations in architecture can be seen.

The architectural critic Martin Pawley draws a comparison with modern advertisements: the modern car standing nonchalantly in front of a stately home is seen by the prospective purchaser as having an association with the pedigree, prestige, quality, and affluence of the historic house. Subliminally, the car 'is invisible, what they see are images of old money, not pictures of new cars'.[12]

A central issue is this: how clearly should the references be stated; to what extent should they be understood by the observer? A small detail in Terry Farrell's restoration scheme for the Seven Dials site in Covent Garden serves as a simple starting point to explore the question. He uses, in the balustrading for the scheme, the motif of a 'C' joined to a reversed 'C'. To some, this motif will remain an unnoticed detail; others, however, may consciously note the deliberate play on the client's name Comyn Ching; others may pick up the reference subliminally. The company has used the site for decades as a retail warehouse for the ironmongery trade, they are part of the history of the site. Farrell's anecdotal detail forms an incidental association between the new work and the history of the site. The level of recognition is less important; what matters is that a statement of association has been made.

Farrell uses the same process at the TV AM building at Camden. Here he transforms what would historically be a series of classical urns along the skyline into a series of 'eggs sitting in eggcups'. At one level they remain classical urns; at another level they make reference to 'breakfast television'. This association was not designed as a heavyweight theoretical stance but as an amusing gesture. Nevertheless, it has become a popular image, a successful logo.

These are incidental details, nevertheless, the associations they form are real. They illustrate the process.

3.6 Levels of comprehension

The process can work at various levels of comprehension. Consider, for example, the sea sculptures of Eduardo Chillida.[13] His large iron structures which project defiantly out of the cliff rocks at Donostia Bay, San Sebastian, Spain, are powerful, yet ambiguous. It is reasonable to deduce that their position, robustness, and shape form an association with the power of the waves, the force of the wind, and the strength of the rocks in resisting these forces. Does it matter that the observer may not be aware, also, of Chillida's use of these pieces as a statement, an association, a reference to the strength of the Basque people and their resistance to external political pressures? The sculptures can work at either level; the associations are similar. The ambiguity enhances their quality.

Similarly, Chillida's sculptural intervention in the historic square at Vitoria, Gasteiz, Spain (Fig. 3.2) shows that same subtlety; it has that same rich range of meaning. He was commissioned to provide a piece of sculpture for the square: he chose to dominate the whole area with large, abstracted, stone landscape walls. These obviously have an association with 'basement ruins' and 'historic fortification'. It is questionable whether the degree of abstraction in the shape of the landscape walls is sufficient for the observer to realise that they are in fact a pretence of the history rather than a reconstruction of history. Putting this aside

Figure 3.2. Vitoria Square, Gasteiz, Spain. Eduardo Chillida's sculptural intervention recalls both the idea of castle basements and the strength of the Basque people. (photograph courtesy of Eduardo Chillida)

for later discussion (see section 7.5, 'Building history'), the association is nevertheless strong. Again, it is not important that the observer may not immediately be aware that these sculptural statements also form a link with the trials of personal strength so loved by the Basque people. The sculptural intervention not only provides areas for tug-of-war, lifting of great weights, and playing pelota, but also stimulates an echo of similar characteristics through the thickness and shape of these heavyweight stone 'fortifications'.

Another example is the Jubilee Sea Swimming Pool at Penzance. This, Britain's largest outdoor swimming pool, was designed in 1934 by the town's borough engineer, who, it is said, was inspired by the image of a seagull alighting on the water. It is situated at a prominent site within the town's conservation area, and in front of the important view across to St Michael's Mount. The people like the pool,[14] they feel that it is appropriate for its location. Again, it does not matter how directly or indirectly the designer's intention is understood.

This layering of comprehension enhances the architecture. It needs, however, to be crafted at a subtle and intelligent level. The mere use of an architectural pun is not good enough: the architectural equivalent of 'when is a door not a door, when it's a jar' is banal. The naïve architectural pun fails because, unlike the child's joke, it cannot be put aside. Architecture cannot be put away; it is permanent.

This sense of reality veiled by references and allegory is central to Italo Calvino's book *Invisible Cities* (Calvino 1972). The reader is transported through cities portrayed as 'a ship that will take us away'[15] or, as 'a city of twists and turns from a dream chase of a woman with long hair'.[16] He makes images from lists of city symbols:

> The man who knows how Zora is made can imagine he is walking along the streets and he remembers the order by which the copper clock follows the barber's striped awning, then the fountain, the astronomer's glass tower, the melon vendor's kiosk, the statue of the hermit, and the turkish bath.[17]

Although Calvino's interwoven associations fail to define the hard factual data of the cities, they do achieve an accurate perception of what the city is about, what it feels like, its culture and its characteristics. It is these city symbols which trigger our memory, these are the references that form our associations.

Again, the various urban spaces created in Giorgio de Chirico's paintings are not accurate representations of the real world, they stimulate associations of space, of wandering in an indeterminate volume. Yet in spite of this vagueness, the sensations are vivid and strong. There is a similar sense of searching and feeling for space in the modern paintings of Harriet Mena Hill.[18]

3.7 Layers of meaning

What happens when more than one reference is stated on the same building? Literature serves as a useful analogy.

The following lines from *Antony and Cleopatra* demonstrate Shakespeare's use of word associations which flow quickly from one image to another.[19]

> *Antony:* O sun, thy uprise shall I see no more!
> Fortune and Antony part here; even here
> Do we shake hands. – All come to this? – The hearts
> That spaniel'd me at heels, to whom I gave
> Their wishes, do discandy, melt their sweets
> On blossoming Caesar; and this pine is bark'd
> That overtopp'd them all.[20]

The writing of Umberto Eco serves as a source to explore the problems encountered when several references are used simultaneously. He delights in constructing a labyrinth of ideas; he describes his novel *Foucault's Pendulum* as 'consisting of an irresponsible interplay of ideas and using copious flashback'.[21] Literature allows this complex duplicity of references to exist, the mind's eye can flit from one image to another. In architecture, however, the image is static, immutable, the references stand permanently together. This is not to say that a building cannot be read in several ways, that it cannot have several meanings, but that it is necessary to recognise that these several references coexist, they stand side by side, to form a single permanent and unalterable totality. They cannot, as in literature, be alternated, switched from one image to the other.

The conundrum is illustrated in Peter Behren's famous AEG Turbine Hall in Berlin. He uses a modern version of the formal pedimented classical facade for the Huttenstrasse frontage. Yet he describes the detailing of the corner panelling of this facade as lightweight metal frames covered externally with horizontally grooved cement rendering to express that they are non-loadbearing elements over the building's heavy structural frame. How can these same corner panels also form what must be interpreted as a reference to the loadbearing columns of the classical facade?[22] Whether or not this conflict was intentional can be debated, the point is to recognise that there is a danger in the use of several references within the same building, and that it is necessary for the designer to ensure that they work together. It is a rewarding but dangerous game.

It is easier in music where, for example, Vaughan Williams runs two sound images simultaneously in the motet *Lord, Thou Hast Been Our Refuge*. This makes use of the duality of his setting of psalm 90 and Croft's fine hymn tune *St Anne* for Isaac Watts's words *O God, Our Help in Ages Past*. The two images strengthen each other, the juxtaposition of the modern and the traditional settings enhance their distinctive characteristics.

This duplication of references and meaning tends to thicken the ambiguity. Umberto Eco accepts this, he recognises that *Foucault's Pendulum*, like his previous historical novel *The Name of the Rose*, is scarcely designed to be logical to any but a few readers. What matters, he says, is for the reader to 'realise that it simply isn't necessary to understand all the references but to respond to the way in which it touches contemporary chords'.[23]

This again can be extended into music where, as an example, John Holloway's music for the modern opera *Clarissa*[24] makes use of several historical references.

The music is overtly modern yet contains undercurrents of Wagner, Debussy, and Schumann. These are not historical quotations but layers of sound in the spirit of these composers. They are not used to give the music some sort of academic pedigree, but to generate appropriate associations with the inner experiences of the over-life-size qualities of the central characters.[25] It does not matter that each reference is not individually recognised; it is the spirit of the historical associations which 'touches the contemporary chords'.

It seems reasonable for this to apply to architecture. References within a building need not be explicitly understood. It is acceptable for the accumulative architectural statement to convey only the spirit of the association. This is seen in Terry Farrell's work at Tobacco Dock, Wapping. The new architectural elements added to the early nineteenth-century warehouse for its conversion into a shopping centre are detailed, not as replicas of nineteenth-century construction, but as modern elements in the spirit of warehouse construction. The new shopfronts (Fig. 3.3), balustrades, and light fittings are obviously modern, yet they contain references to the innovative industrial construction used by Alexander and Rennie for the original building.

It could be argued that, to be made aware of the details of each historical reference may in fact detract from the observer's appreciation of the overall spirit of the association. Knowledge of the specific may rivet the observer's consciousness; the observer may see only the detailed historical image rather than the suggested, and required, characteristic image.

Quinlan Terry's proposed new library for Downing College, Cambridge, raises these questions. He was faced with the difficult task of placing the new Maitland Robinson Library building within the strong context of William Wilkins's neo-classical college. Quinlan Terry chose a historical approach for the design of the new library, but not one which aped the severity of Wilkins's Greek revival buildings. The design is basically a 'pavilion' to be seen in the round with its various parts adopting different historical references, a historical 'capriccio' based on the typology of a Palladian villa. The south portico takes its detailed reference from the Theseion, Athens; the east portico from the Choragic Monument of Thrasyilus; and, rising from the centre of the roof, is a structure referenced from the Tower of the Winds, Athens. This interesting design raises certain questions. Is this collection of references seen as a historical catalogue or does it form some kind of mental association? If so, what is this association? Is there an association between Quinlan Terry's new building and some intellectual idea about classicism? These questions hinge on the type of image being formed. Does the observer see a series of fixed physical images of specific Greek buildings, or rather an indeterminate image of antiquity?

3.8 Translation of ideas into architecture

The problem is that you cannot build 'emotion', although you can imply it; you cannot use 'foggy' bricks or 'sad' timber. It is possible to produce an emotional drawing but this does not help towards the physical construction of feelings.

Figure 3.3. Tobacco Dock, Wapping, London. Terry Farrell. New shopfronts detailed to reflect the industrial nature of the original building. (photograph James Strike)

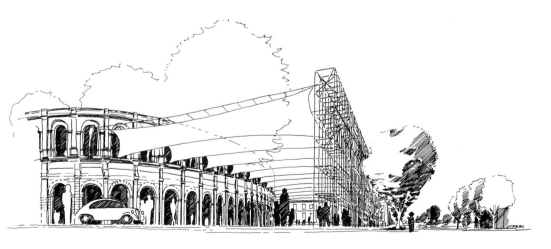

Figure 3.4. Place des Arènes, Nîmes, France. Architect Cezary Bednarski, structural engineer Peter Higson. Proposal for a cover of canvas sails designed as an unthreatening, lightweight, temporary construction. (drawing Cezary Bednarski)

Jonathan Miller's analytical thought helps to identify the way associations are formed. In 1989 he took part in the Folio Society Debate 'Good literature is too substantial to fit through the lens of a camera'.[26] He identified two types of visual image: the 'determinate image' and the 'indeterminate image'. He equates the 'determinate image' with that which we see on a photograph or the film screen, these are physical images that, even if the photograph is vague or shadowy, are still generated from each and every physical item in front of the camera. He equates 'indeterminate image' with our visual interpretation of literature – mental images, which may be vivid, but also remain incomplete in certain respects.

The difference between the two types of image is seen when literature is translated into film. Miller suggests that the translation suffers in two ways. It suffers through 'the sins of commission', that is, the image encompasses too much information, it becomes too determinate:

> You can sustain, for example, a vivid image of Mr Carker's teeth in *Dombey and Son* without having to visualise the rest of Mr Carker's face. The bother is that when you have it on film the rest of Mr Carker has boringly and unremittingly got to be there, as long as he's on screen.[27]

It suffers also through 'the sins of omission':

> Pictures cannot contain what philosophers would call propositional attitudes. You cannot indicate that something is, say, peculiarly repulsive, other than by showing something which is generally agreed to be peculiarly repulsive. In a novel you can indicate that something is repulsive or disgusting or disturbing without there being anything about it that is physically or visually disturbing: you can say 'there was something about the room which disturbed him'.[28]

There are similarities in architecture. The type of image engendered by a piece of architecture influences the type of association formed by the observer. When a designer sets out to form an association between a new building and a particular characteristic, it is necessary for 'the message' of that characteristic to be implanted into the design. The characteristic, whatever it may be, has to be translated, through the design process, from an intellectual idea into the reality of an actual building. In doing so, the designer needs to be aware of the problems of commission and omission. Take, for example, the Tower of the Winds which rises through the roof of Quinlan Terry's new library for Downing College (see section 3.7, 'Layers of meaning'). It is detailed as an exact copy of the Greek tower in Athens; the copy is a total commission of the original building. The observer is thus given a determinate image of the actual Greek building which you see on your way up to the Acropolis. The observer thus forms an association between the new library building and the Greek tower in Athens. If, however, the designer's intention had been to encourage some form of association with the characteristics of the Tower of the Winds, related, say, to the original Andronikos Cyrrhestes horological water clock and sundial, and to the subliminal ideas of time, direction, and history, then the detailing for the new library would need to be more suggestive, more symbolic, more implicit, less explicit, less determinate. The aim being to stimulate a connection with the spirit of the Tower of the Winds rather than to produce a replica of it: to create an indeterminate image of the Greek horological tower.

The architectural sin of omission, in translation of an intellectual idea into the reality of a building, presents a greater problem. Feelings cannot be physically translated into architecture. The only hope is to find some symbolic gesture which moves the observer in the right direction.

A project which moves towards the difficult task of implying an emotion is the proposed scheme for a new library in Alexandria, Egypt. The UNESCO competition was won by the architectural group Snohetta of Norway. Their design has a spiritual quality which arises from the strong circular geometry of the scheme. The large, top-lit circular drum of the library hall, which tilts through the surface of the ground, has been described as looking both 'forward and backward in time',[29] while the inclined enclosing wall, faced with scriptures carved in stone relief, similarly face outwards to 'nature' and, below ground, face inward to 'human creativity'. The question arises as to how far this emotional response is triggered by the project itself or from the project's own history; the seat of learning since Alexander the Great, the place of the calculations of the circumference and tilt of the earth by Eratosthenes, the rules of anatomy by Herophilus, the philosophy of Plotinus, the reordering of the map of the world by Ptolemy; let alone the controversy about the end of the ancient Bibliotheca Alexandria.

3.9 The significance of time

It is interesting to observe that temporary constructions are normally formed using lightweight tenuous engineering. We still associate such structures as being temporary; as opposed to the permanance of heavy compressive structures. Perhaps the increase in the number of permanent tensile structures now being built will gradually erode this perception. However, the point here is that this perception of tensile structures being temporary renders them less threatening at historic sites. The large concert stage constructed each summer for the evening concerts at Marble Hill House, Twickenham, would stimulate far more objection if it were not a temporary structure. The stage is located close to the river Thames on the central axis of the house. There could not be a more contentious location for a structure large enough to enclose a full concert orchestra. Seen in the context of the summer evening gala, this is modern and exhilarating, especially when lit up at night.

An elegant temporary structure is proposed for a cover over the Arena site in Nîmes, France (Fig. 3.4). This stands confidently alongside the Roman amphitheatre, but in no way threatens it. It is particularly lightweight, reminiscent of summer sunshades hung in the trees. It confirms the impression that it is temporary and will soon be taken down. Other lightweight structures, designed as permanent installations, can make use of this response and thus appear less threatening (see Figs 3.1 and 5.14).

What is of importance to this study is that the static nature of a building prevents the symbolism and meaning of the architecture from changing. It is a once and for ever statement (see section 3.7, 'Layers of meaning'). Jonathan Miller's classification of images (section 3.8) would describe architecture as 'determinate' with each and every physical item in the observer's eye.

This permanence presents a problem at this time in history when the design world is preoccupied with images that flash momentarily in front of the consumer. Gombrich, writing about the psychology of pictorial representation, refers to our age thus:

> Never before has there been an age like ours when the visual image was so cheap in every sense of the word. We are surrounded and assailed by posters and advertisements, by comics and magazine illustrations.[30]

Images of international wars are followed on the television screen by pictures of people eating bowls of cereal. The screen is unable to assign them a sense of priority.

To complicate the matter further, it has been noted (see section 2.1, 'Views of history') that attitudes towards conservation, and thus attitudes towards the way we respond to the architectural symbols and associations, change gradually over the decades. How then are we to use associations in new architecture to help the new building to exist sympathetically alongside historic fabric?

The inherent difficulty should not be seen as a reason for avoiding the issue. There are so many pieces of new architecture that fail because of this lack of commitment or sheer ignorance of the possibilities. There are, however, two suggestions which may be helpful. First, it is necessary to work with associations that link with long-term issues rather than with ephemeral ideas. Second, it is better to form the association with the history of the site, or the actual historic fabric, rather than the present or proposed use of the buildings. The new design intervention at the Natural History Museum for example (see Fig. 6.16) forms a strong and well-detailed association with the biological use of the new ecology display to the detriment of its relationship with Waterhouse's fine building.

Finally, time gives to architecture a long-term levelling effect. The process of ageing through exposure to the elements and general wear and tear gives buildings a patina which camouflages the differences of new and old. The levelling effect towards some form of collective ambience comes also from the familiarity of the buildings; the shock of the new recedes and is replaced in the long term by a degree of acceptance. As buildings get older they gradually become part of a common group; the older they are, the stronger the commonality becomes. We see the muddle of properties of different periods in the village as being of one history.

4

Response to location

This chapter considers how the location and setting of a historic building can influence the design of a new piece of architecture needed for the site. It explores this relationship between the new and the old; ideas which may be used to stimulate the design of the new architecture. It considers these design concepts under separate headings but, in doing so, it recognises that they may be related, connected, overlaid. It is for the designer to take the overview, to interpret and evaluate the priorities.

This chapter is, therefore, concerned with 'a sense of place': how we evaluate and respond to the spaces in and around our sites. We need not be put off by such academic terms as 'ecoanalysis of places',[1] but we should recognise these ideas as components in the formulation of the brief for the future of a site.

4.1 Historical tracks and paths

A farmer walks across the grassland to tend his cattle. The daily steps become a track, and progressive journeys turn this into a footpath. The path becomes known as part of the matrix of routes across the area. Local trade, regional politics, power struggles, and religion cause the movement of people, cattle, wagons, traders, and even armies across the countryside. Paths, valley slopes, and river crossings link up into routes and roads. Fortifications, buildings for trade, resting houses, and places of worship are constructed along these routes. It is these places that we now see as historic sites.

Many of our historic sites hold a specific relationship with this matrix of tracks, paths, and roads. People who now come to these historic sites probably use, perhaps unwittingly, part of this system of ancient routes. The site plans of these historical areas may now appear complicated but, nevertheless, certain characteristics do recur. Consider, for example, how hospice buildings, places of rest, and chantry chapels usually stand close by the side of pilgrim ways and long-distance routes; these are wayside buildings to serve the wayfarer. Similarly, lines of defence stand across routes, at right angles to them; gate-houses and city gates straddle across the routes. And look-out towers and artillery positions command high ground, located to overlook the route. Although the relationship is obvious at certain sites, it can also be discovered as an undercurrent where changes and subsequent buildings have gradually obscured the original building or route. Dover Castle and the Pharos light stand on high ground, obviously, as a guard for the channel sea route. On a smaller scale, St John's Chapel, Ely (now an agricultural barn), stands as a hospice for travellers alongside the ancient route into the city. However, it needs a historical perspective to see Temple Manor at Strood, not only as an old house in the middle of an industrial estate, but also as one of several lodging houses for the Knights Templars alongside the route through Rochester and Dover on their way to and from the Holy Land.

It is necessary for the designer to establish how the existing building relates to the specific pattern of routes in the area, and then to decide what role the new architecture is playing to strengthen this relationship. How will the visitors see the site and the new architecture as they pass along the ancient tracks? Do they perceive it as a gateway to be passed through; as a porter's lodge, or toll house at the side of the road; or as a look-out tower or folly high on the top of the hill? That they are different is seen in the words we use; towers *stand* on hill tops and croft houses *lie* in valleys.[2]

Each of these relationships is different, each requires a different approach to the location of the new architecture. Working through some examples helps to flesh out the idea.

A simple case is the entrance to Carisbrooke Castle on the Isle of Wight. An improvement was needed for the existing ticket kiosk, which was really no more than an overheated perspex box. Looking for a rationale for the design of a new office led to the realisation that, from a historical point of view, there would not have been a building at this strategic defensive position outside the gate. It was therefore decided to remove the inappropriate kiosk and provide custodial facilities within the historic fabric on the inner side of the gate.

A clear and neat example of new architecture built on an old route is the new Visitors' Centre on the approach to the small and unspoilt fishing harbour of Clovelly in North Devon (Fig. 4.1). The new building, which is not without hints of nautical tradition, stands on the track leading down to the village. Visitors leave their cars and walk through the new building. It becomes part of the experience of descending to the harbour. Similarly, the new Visitors' Centre for Fountains Abbey, Yorkshire, is also placed along the route up to the monument. Here the approach up to the Abbey is carefully manipulated: the visitor is first introduced to a distant sight of the tower, then taken on a route of 'serendipity', through views and glimpses which unfold and close as the visitor moves up towards and through the new centre. The new building, by Edward Cullinan (see Fig. 4.15), is axially aligned on to the imposing tower yet hidden from the Abbey grounds by the slope of the ground.

Peter Eisenman's scheme for the Centre for the Visual Arts at the Ohio State University combines the use of route with a recall of local history (Fig. 4.2). A new pedestrian route, which is angled to the grid of the city streets, cuts through the existing university buildings. This, together with the circulation route which

Figure 4.1. Visitors' Centre, Clovelly, North Devon. Van Heyningen and Haward's new facilities designed as part of the pedestrian route down to the harbour. (photograph van Heyningen and Haward)

crosses it at right angles, sets the dynamic geometry of the scheme. The entrance to the pedestrian route is accentuated by a modern interpretation of the old Armory buildings which used to be on the site. The new centre is to house avant-garde and experimental arts; it is not a repository for traditional art. Eisenman interprets:

> The new crossing which we have created as an intersection of the two 'found' axes is not simply a route, but an event, literally a *centre* for the visual arts. We believe that our proposal represents an aesthetic that is consonant with the programme. At the same time it responds sensitively to the history and context of the campus.[3]

Terry Farrell's scheme for the development of Charing Cross railway station, London, responds to its location at the end of a route. Although the new building is much taller than a conventional train shed, it retains a similar form of a terminus for the rail tracks which cross over the river into central London. The use of this type of 'functional-loci' design device can, however, lead to misrepresentation. The Alban Gate office development in the Barbican area of London is successful as a modern expression of a gateway, but gives a false impression of the past. Its position near the centre, rather than on the boundary wall, of the second-century Roman fort should not be portrayed as a position of a gate into the city.

Nicoletti's winning design for the new museum at the Acropolis, Athens, is a fascinating example (Fig. 4.3). The scheme, located at the base of the Acropolis, responds in various ways to its historical and topographical location. Like the Visitors' Centre at Fountains Abbey, it also allows for a sense of serendipity in the visitors' path up to the site. Views of the Parthenon are forced into the heart of the new museum so that the visitor sees the archaeological artefacts that relate to the site against a backdrop of the actual site. Visitors are then sent forward along a carefully turned route from which the Parthenon slowly comes into view.

The designer needs to position the new building with great care, the slightest shift could spoil its correct allegiance to the existing matrix of historic buildings and paths. The historical characteristics of each location can be used to generate the new design. These ideas are not to do with style, they can be used to generate either modern architecture or a historical scheme, the design generators remain the same.

4.2 External spaces

One of the joys of walking around historic areas is to experience the diversity of open space which exists between the buildings. The variation is enormous, ranging, for example, from the flat open river flood plain in front of Newark Castle, to the tight narrow alleyways threading through the Lanes of Brighton. The shape of the space may be as symmetrical as the quads of Oxford University, or as odd as the medieval market square of the Suffolk town of Clare (see section

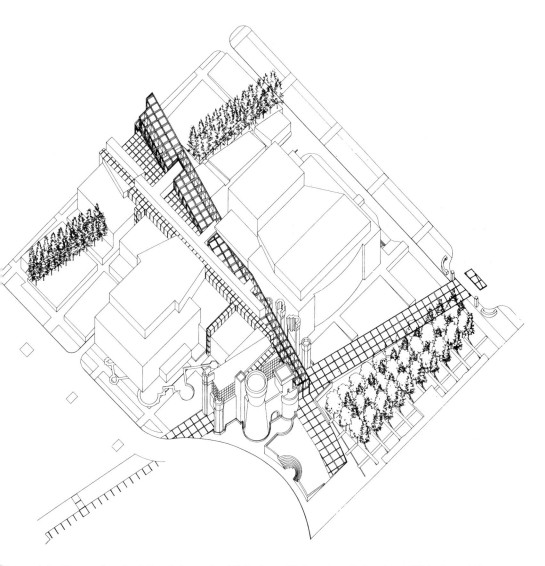

Figure 4.2. Centre for the Visual Arts, the Ohio State University, Columbus, USA. Peter Eisenman with Robertson, Trott and Bean. Scheme generated from the existing routes through the site. (reproduced from *Architectural Design*)

4.6, 'Grain and matrix'). The space may have a particular geometry, such as the distinctive scalloped fan shape of the Campo in Sienna, or the foreshortened perspective of the Capitol at Rome.

There is also variation in the way these spaces link together. It is a delight to walk through the different piazzas in the Italian town of Mantua, strung together via narrow alleyways and open spaces joined corner to corner.

The particular characteristics of these historic spaces contribute to the distinctive quality of each site. It is important for the designer to study these characteristics and decide how the new piece of architecture is able to enhance the quality of the existing spaces.

The scheme by Leon Krier for New College, Oxford (regrettably abandoned) would have made a valuable contribution to the urban space. The proposal (Fig. 4.4) was to use the new blocks to transform the existing vague and open spaces into a well-defined public square. Between the two blocks would have been a tight wedge of private space. Krier envisages an urban transition between the grandeur of the university's Central Buildings and the suburban aspect of Victorian and Edwardian north Oxford. The New College group, and the new alley of trees along Savile Road, would have completed an articulate and varied enclosure.[4]

Initial schemes to insert a new building for the Institute of Archaeological Research into North Court of the Downing Site, Cambridge, indicated that the required volume would be too big for the space available. The new building had either to block across the centre of the existing space to form two smaller courts (see Forbes Mellon Library, Fig. 4.5) or stand centrally within the court like a piece of sculpture to be seen in the round. The linear assembly of T. G. Jackson's north, east, and west elevations, 1904–11, made it impossible to break in for a cross-court insertion, so a sculpture-like building had to be designed with its footprint reduced by placing some of the accommodation below ground with 'garden features' providing top light. The strategy was sucessfully realised by the Casson Conder Partnership.

4.3 Formal and informal sites

Some sites are inherently formal, the buildings ordered and the spaces they enclose regular. It should not be assumed, however, that the classification 'formal site' simply means a 'classical site'. Many sites made up of classical buildings have, for all sorts of historical quirks, evolved over the years into informal groupings; and, of course, many formal spaces are enclosed within non-classical buildings. Formal spaces have also been formed within natural land-scapes through formal planting or the modelling of the ground such as the Tilt Yard at Dartington, or the enclosures within many of our formal gardens. It is worth recalling that the early Greek sites were distinctly informal, the buildings placed in a natural response to need and to the local terrain. It was not until the mid-fifth century BC that they adopted the 'gridiron' system of city planning.

Figure 4.3. The Acropolis Museum, Athens. Manfredi Nicoletti and Studio Passarelli. View looking down from the Acropolis. The glass roof allows the visitors to see the museum exhibits against the backdrop of the actual site. (drawing Manfredi Nicoletti)

Compare, for example, the city plan of Thasos with the city plan of Miletus as rebuilt following its destruction by the Persians in 494 BC.[5] The importance of the sites, in this context, is that they are formal, not that they are classical.

It is interesting to speculate on the changes planned by Charles II for the city of Winchester. His desire for a fashionable formal route from the Cathedral up to the Castle Hall would have carved a swath of axial formality through what we now see as a medieval street pattern.

Other sites are inherently informal: the buildings, built at various times and of differing architectural styles, do not conform to an overall plan. The resultant spaces between the buildings are irregular and unpredictable. Some spaces are deliberately planned to be informal, such as the picturesque grouping of Blaise Hamlet in Bristol or the sways and gentle arcs used in 1950s housing estates.

These historical characteristics of the site, formal or informal, need to be taken into account when considering the location, planning, and design of the new piece of architecture. The new architecture needs to contribute to the specific characteristic of the site. Normally, this will be either by the strengthening of its formality or by a contribution to its asymmetric informality.

Consider some examples. The lightweight cover proposed to stand alongside the Roman Amphitheatre in Nîmes makes a contribution to the shape of the Place des Arènes (see Fig. 3.4). The design by Cezary Bednarski (structural engineer Peter Higson) creates both a line of supports to square up and regularise the area, and a series of sails which float gently up to the curve of the amphitheatre.

The Roman camp of Chesters Fort on Hadrian's Wall is made up of formal Roman planning. In 1903 a small museum, designed by Norman Shaw, was built at the entrance to the site, and in the 1960s a visitors' centre was built close to this museum. It seems somewhat strange that the visitors' centre was positioned at a slight cant to the museum – perhaps it followed the line of an incidental fence which has since been removed. Whatever the reason, the space created between the two buildings is unsatisfactory. In 1988 a scheme was prepared to enlarge the museum. This presented two problems: how to deal with the unresolved space between the buildings, and how to retain the integrity of Norman Shaw's 'Tuscan' gem as a small object in its own right. The proposed scheme makes the space into a formal square, it re-establishes the formal characteristic of the site by making reference to the idea of the Roman courtyard (see Fig. 7.3).

Arup Associates not only solved the problem of finding space for a new building in Cambridge, but in doing so they created two tight, but well-formed courtyards out of the existing larger L-shaped space of Memorial Court, Clare College. The new Forbes Mellon Library (Fig. 4.5) successfully resolves the existing space into two formal areas. The apparent volume of the smaller court is increased by the beautifully detailed arcade which takes its reference from the Pazzi Chapel in the cloister of Santa Croce, Florence.

The Arche de la Défense, Paris, is generated by its formal location. The design is

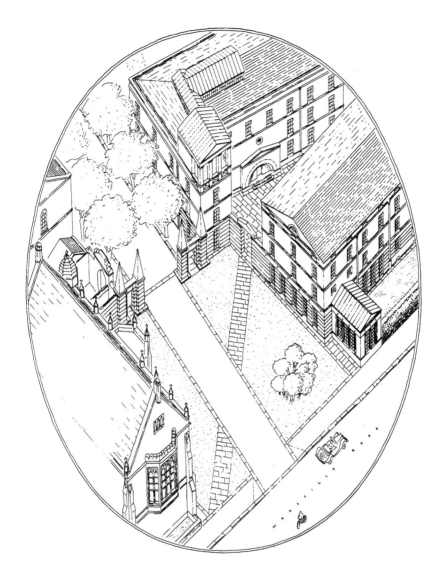

Figure 4.4. New College, Oxford. Leon Krier in partnership with John Robins. The new accommodation resolves the space between the existing buildings into a series of tight informal enclosures. (reproduced from *Architect's Journal*)

derived from the formal axial plan from the Louvre and the Arc de Triomphe which it extends and strengthens.

The Louvre project, by I. M. Pei, also responds to its location with the formality of the new glass pyramid reflecting the formality of the square in which it stands. This is slightly diminished by the size and number of surrounding pools and fountains, which reduce the surface area of the original paving to such an extent as to diminish the quality of the horizontal plane of the historic space.[6] Pei's intervention caused much controversy when it first appeared, but it soon found public acclaim. The pyramid development unlocks the circulation problem in the Louvre museum, particularly in access and refurbishment of the basement vaults. The glass for the pyramid was specially developed by Saint Gobain to conform to Pei's demand for a 'pure white' transparency without a hint of the green tinge of normal toughened glass. The pyramid is never a solid object but more a filter through which one can still see the historic fabric.

An example of a new piece of architecture used to enhance the asymmetry of the site is Derek Latham's scheme for the extension and conversion of the Old Mill at Oundle, Northamptonshire (Fig. 4.6). The new extension for the conversion of the mill into a hotel resolves the disparate lines of the curved millpond, the existing buildings, and angle of the road.

This is not to say that a designer could not use new architecture as a deliberate antithesis of the existing formal, or informal, characteristics of the site. This requires a clear understanding of the issues: however, one step towards making this work is to ensure that the new architecture makes a clear and separate visual statement. The Junior Common Room at Keble College, Oxford (Fig. 4.7), is a successful example. The new common room, designed by Ahrens Burton and Koralek, forms a coil which is placed confidently within Butterfield's orthogonal plan. It makes a clear statement between that which is formal and that which breaks away from the right angle. A similarity can be seen in literature where, for example, a break from the formality of conventional grammar can be used to make a particular point or a literary gesture. What is important is that the author writes the passage in such a way as to convey to the reader that it was a deliberate break from the conventional rules and not just a lazy mistake.

The designer needs to look at the planning of the locality to establish how the new architecture can contribute to the inherent characteristics.

This is a useful moment to explore the analytical technique of 'figure' and 'field'. This is a particularly useful device for exploring the design concept of formality (and informality), although of course it can equally be used in other forms of analysis. The idea is to use a device that stimulates a visual interplay between buildings and external spaces, between solid and void, between figure and field. The technique was explored by the artist Matisse.[7] His use of flat painted planes and patterns is seen as early as 1911 in such paintings as *Nature morte, Seville 1*. This process evolved in his mural *La danse 1*, 1931–2, to the extent that the subject (that is the dancer) is no longer the figure of the work; the canvas has become an amalgam of both the figure and the field in which it stands.

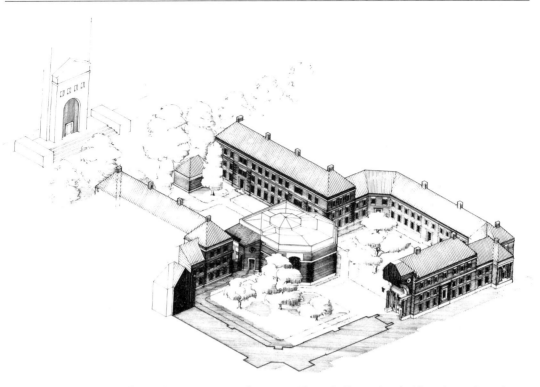

Figure 4.5. Forbes Mellon Library, Memorial Court, Clare College, Cambridge. Arup Associates. The new building divides the existing L-shaped space into two small formal courts. (drawing Arup Associates)

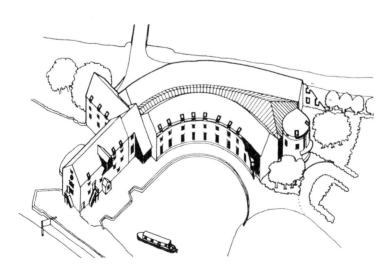

Figure 4.6. The Old Mill, Oundle, Northamptonshire. Derek Latham's proposed extension responds to the curvature of the river. (drawing Derek Latham and Associates)

47

By 1952 *Nu bleu* has achieved a clear sense of interplay between the figure and the field; between the physical presence of the body and the enveloping negative areas. In architectural terms, the technique can be explored by reversing the building parts of the plan for the spaces which exist around them. A conventional plan thus becomes inverted to a figure ground plan (see Fig. 4.8). This technique allows the interplay between buildings and spaces to be examined. The external space becomes, for a moment, the primary object of critical attention.

This reversal of solid and void is used by the sculptor Rachel Whiteread. Her work for her nomination for the 1992 Turner Art Prize included a large solid white object formed from the whole interior cubic space within a domestic bed-sitting room. The sculpture gives a new perspective on the volumes in which we live.

4.4 Layers of history

Palimpsest is a useful word: 'a parchment on which two or more texts have been written, each text effaced to make room for the next' (Greek: *palim* – again, *psestos* – rubbed smooth). Many historic sites have these same characteristics, the existing buildings stand on the ground of previous buildings which have been removed.

Over the years the use of a building may change, the architectural style may become unfashionable, the size of the court may increase, living patterns change, fortifications become necessary. What we now see is a 'palimpsest' of history, signs of previous change, evidence of previous defensive ditches, clues of discarded walls, remnants of abandoned outbuildings. The layers of history are visible for those who look. The evidence can also be traced and established through historical research: maps, documents, literature, works of art, all help to piece together the history of the site.

The evidence of different historical periods remains visible at many sites. At Gloucester Blackfriars, for example, the change after the Reformation from monastic church to residential use caused the unusual juxtaposition of domestic sash windows inserted into the great Gothic transept wall. This layering often leaves us with the remains of historical fragments which appear tantalisingly unresolved, built around and absorbed into the more recent history as a patina and story-board of the past.

The layering is not always immediately visible. A visitor to Greys Court at Henley-on-Thames first sees a picturesque group of buildings, a typical English assortment of buildings. It takes time to realise that beneath this apparently informal group lies a fourteenth-century, four square castellated mansion with its four defensive towers and fortified walls. The line of the walls can be traced in the dry season across the lawns. This understanding of the site not only stimulates greater enjoyment of the visit, but also helps to make sense of the existing buildings.

Figure 4.7. Junior Common Room, Keble College, Oxford. Ahrens Burton and Koralek. (a) The lower level of glazing sweeps out to enclose an asymmetric curved space. (b) View towards Butterfield's college chapel.

New architecture can respond to this evolutionary process. It can be seen as a reformation of an earlier layer, a previous condition of the site used to generate the design of the new architecture. The new architecture thus becomes a recasting of lost fabric, not as a replica of the old buildings, but as a memory of the earlier buildings. It makes use of their location, the spirit of their form, and their typology. The new Haas Haus shopping centre in Vienna makes use of this idea (Fig. 4.9). The new buildings by Hans Hollein reconstruct the line of the now vanished city wall close to St Stephen's Cathedral. The buildings along the Graben break down to reveal a mirror glass outline of the medieval city wall and bastion. This idea is also used to form the central plaza of the new Civic Centre at Tsukuba, Japan. Here, Arata Isozaki's composition uses layers of reconstructed history, with each terrace level taking its reference from a different historical motif. The deepest layer is based on Michelangelo's perspective paving for the Campidoglio in Rome; subsequent levels use free interpretation of classical themes; while the top terrace is paved with a modern tartan planning grid.

Kevin Lynch, in *What Time is this Place?*, writes: 'The aesthetic aim is to make visual the process of change'.[8] And Timothy Gray, a student under Randolph Langenbach at the Department of Architecture, University of California, Berkeley, proposes a design theory for new architecture based on an additive layered approach which he calls 'designing without erasing'.[9]

It is this layering of history which prompts us to dig up the past: there is a natural curiosity to strip off each layer to discover what lies beneath. The simplistic idea that deeper is both older and of more value is mocked by the quip 'the most ancient civilisation in London must therefore be the Piccadilly tube trains'! Fortunately, new attitudes towards research and methods of investigation have reduced the amount of damage. The abandoned site of the Roman city of Italica in Spain, for example, is now being mapped by a joint team of British and Spanish archaeologists using non-destructive, ground-penetrating radar.[10] The moral question is illustrated at the Abbey of St Mary Grace on the Royal Mint Site opposite the Tower of London. Was it acceptable to destroy the Victorian brick floors of the victualling yards, and evidence of the Georgian basements, to get down to the medieval ruins? Two issues arise as far as new architecture is concerned. First, what to do with the uncovered remains, a problem which frequently calls for a new protective cover structure to form a suitable micro-climate over the remains (see section 5.4, 'Enclosures'). And second, how will the building and presentation of the exposed remains be funded?

4.5 Allegiance of the new architecture

Most buildings belong to a group of buildings; there are few that stand as a single building isolated in the landscape. The planning issue here is for the designer to establish which group of buildings the new architecture is to be attached to.

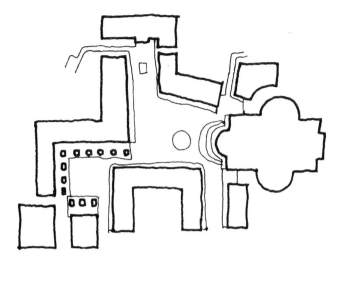

Figure 4.8. 'Conventional' plan transposed into a 'figure ground' plan. (diagram James Strike)

This may be explored through the question: Is the new piece of architecture 'the last building of the village' or 'a gateway to the monument'? This is illustrated diagrammatically in Fig. 4.10, where the facilities move from the village to the historic site. The planning issue is that the design of the new building also changes its allegiance from the planning grain of the village to the curvilinear characteristics of the historic monument.

This is seen at the important neolithic site of Stonehenge, Wiltshire. Here, indeed, is a monument that needs to be seen as a single object in the landscape, seen standing as a remote and strong object in the predominantly featureless landscape[11] (accepting that it is part of a larger archaeological group: the surrounding barrows and circles are of immense historical value, but they do not stand up visually in the landscape like Stonehenge). To erect any new structure as part of the group of standing megaliths would be detrimental to the solemnity of the stones. Article 1 of the Venice Charter states:

> The concept of an historic monument embraces not only the single architectural work but also the urban or rural setting in which is found the evidence of a particular civilisation.

Lowenthal in *The Past is a Foreign Country* describes how 'inaccessibility enhances the mystique of the past'; he quotes Wordsworth, 'secrets older than the flood' and Shelley, 'thrilling secrets of the birth of time', to reach for those feelings associated with such sites.[12]

By the 1960s, visitor numbers at Stonehenge had grown so much that something had to be done. The solution was to provide basic visitor facilities at the site, which, although partially hidden in the ground, were sufficiently close to have a detrimental impact on the monument. The building, and the large car park, created an unwelcome allegiance to the stones. By the 1990s, visitor numbers had increased to six million per year, making the facilities inadequate. Not only had the numbers increased but visitors' expectations of comfort, refreshment, and interpretation of history had also become more demanding. It soon became evident that any new building to satisfy these needs would be too large to be concealed below ground. Something had to be done, and it was realised that the new facilities should change their allegiance away from the stones to the nearby village of Larkhill. This has several advantages: it is easier to design the new facilities as a series of buildings at the edge of the village rather than in the open flat landscape; it makes the monument accessible only to the meaningfully minded who are prepared to walk the half mile from the village to the stones (plus facilities for the disabled); and it allows the stones to stand and be seen in isolation in the landscape.

The idea of new architecture forming an allegiance with a group of buildings can be extended to an allegiance formed with a wider and more abstract historical location. A successful example is the new car park built in the sensitive area just outside the city walls of Chichester. The design by Portchmouth Russum and Birds (see Fig. 6.5) sets up a strong allegiance between the new building and the old city wall. The form and detailing of the new building 'assimilates' the city wall

Figure 4.9. Haas Haus Shopping Centre, Vienna. Hans Hollein. The new building revives the memory of the city wall and bastion. (photograph Richard Bryant/Arcaid)

(see Chapter 6). The round staircase towers and the linear pedestrian walk not only seem like the city wall, but also provide a pleasant route into the city, and form a visual screen to shield the the car park from the city. The second example is Manning and Clamp's Sir Joseph Bank Centre at the Royal Botanic Gardens, Kew, Richmond. This new air-conditioned exhibition and research centre for world timbers is sited in the difficult position between The Herbarium to the east, Kew Palace to the west, the river Thames to the north, and the Botanic Gardens and the Aroid House to the south. It establishes an allegiance with these through its careful siting and design which sinks part of the structure into the ground, uses excavated material for landscape banks and a lake, and a curvilinear patent glazed central concourse evocative of the glasshouses elsewhere in the Gardens (see Fig. 4.11).

4.6 Grain and matrix

English Heritage, in *Conservation Bulletin*, June 1988, state their policy on 'Shopping in historic towns'. This raises concern over the increase in the size and number of new shopping centres being proposed. It recognises that these developments pose a threat to the architectural integrity of our historic towns and cities:

> Once lost, historic character is irretrievable. . . . Many historic town centres could be left as wastelands of disused retail warehouses. Many American towns are bitterly regretting the unplanned destruction of their historic centres.

It goes on to identify the reason why these developments can cause a problem:

> The character of English historic towns derives as much from the continuity of plot size, the survival of back (or burgage) plots, the pattern of lanes and alleys, and the general topography, which make up the 'grain' of the town. . . . The external form of the new structures should seek to minimise the scale and bulk of their internal volumes.

Different towns, and even different areas within a town, have a different type of grain. This change in the topology, matrix of building size, plot size, and street pattern, can be illustrated by comparison of the wide streets and large urban blocks of Berlin, against the intricate and complicated roofscape formed by the tight plots and narrow alleyways of Venice.

It is appropriate for new buildings to respect the existing grain. Erno Goldfinger replicated the grain of the Georgian terraces in the vicinity for his own house Willow Bank in Hampstead. This, an explicit example of the Modern Movement, does not attempt to copy the style of the local houses, only their footprint, volume, and rhythm. Contrast this with the inappropriate bulk of the Podium Shopping Centre in Bath. This new building, located in an architecturally sensitive spot near to Pulteney Bridge, may be detailed with a veneer of neo-classical style, but this does not conceal the monolithic white stone enclosure of a formidable mass.[13]

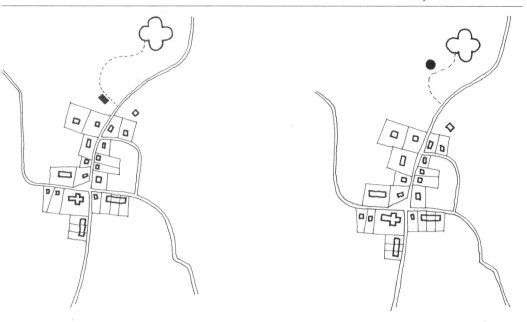

Figure 4.10. A visitors' centre planned as 'the last building of the village', and as 'a gateway to the monument'. (diagram James Strike)

Figure 4.11. Sir Joseph Bank Centre, Royal Botanic Gardens, Kew, London. Manning and Clamp. The landscape responds to its context and the building evokes the memory of Victorian glasshouses. (photograph Manning Clamp and Partners)

55

One of the earliest studies of grain and matrix was *The Anatomy of the Village*, produced by Thomas Sharp in 1946. Chapter 4 in particular identifies different growth patterns of villages and the 'psychology of plan-shapes', by which the distinctive characteristics of 'street', 'square', or 'green' are identified. Sharp recognises that these have to be understood in order to design or criticise new development.

The *Design Framework for Royal Leamington Spa*, produced in 1990 by Rock Townsend for Warwick District Council and English Heritage, aims to provide:

> An awareness of the structure and quality of Leamington Spa as townscape, and the particular architectural quality of its buildings; also, by means of that awareness, to give guidance on the criteria to be applied to development proposals.

This includes an analysis of the various classical set pieces and the different types of residential pattern.

A new scheme which is generated by, and thus responds to the grain of the existing buildings and plots is the new Jocelyn Stevens Arts Centre for the Royal College of Art, Kensington, London (Fig. 4.12). John Miller and Partners' scheme follows the site pattern and the functional simplicity of the service cottages along Jay Mews. It then uses a simple, but effective and useful, clear volume to separate this new construction from the rear of the existing Victorian houses facing on to Queen's Gate. The accommodation makes use of both the new building and these existing houses where the elegant rooms, details, and staircases have been retained. There is, therefore, a pleasing surprise on moving through the new modern detailing to enter the door into the period detailing of the existing staircase wells. You are thus always aware of your position as you move around the accommodation (see section 5.1).

MacCormac Jamieson Prichard use an appropriately tight grain to integrate the new collegiate development of Blue Boar Court into a constrained urban back-land of Cambridge (Fig. 4.13). Small-scale architectural elements are used for the forty-five undergraduate rooms, a common room, and lecture theatre for Trinity College. Raising the college court to first-floor level not only enables this intricate scheme to survive amongst the surounding large buildings, but also provides commercial space at street level for shops and restaurants.

4.7 Regional traditions

Prior to the Industrial Revolution, each region had its own methods of building based on local materials and local methods of construction. It was only the wealthy landowners and the Church who could aspire to new ideas coming in from abroad. These local traditions gave the buildings a regional identity. These regional characteristics are well known and well recorded.[14]

It is frequently stated that new architecture should 'make use of local materials and be sympathetic to local buildings'; such phrases are seen in planning guides

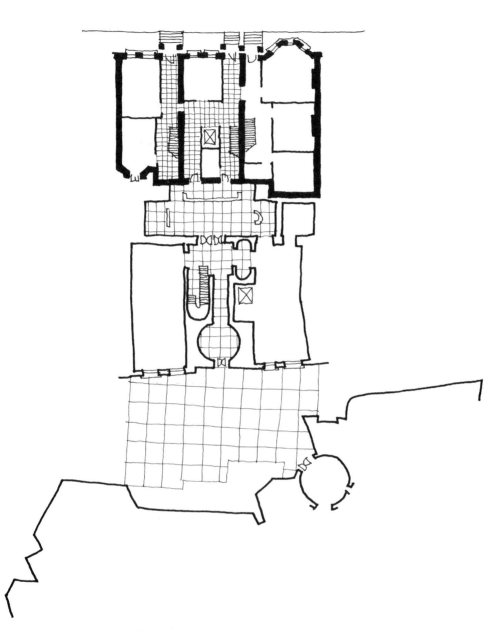

Figure 4.12. Jocelyn Stevens Faculty Building for the Royal College of Art, Kensington, London. John Miller and Partners' scheme stitches together the conflicting size of the existing college, the mews cottages, and the Victorian town houses. (diagram James Strike)

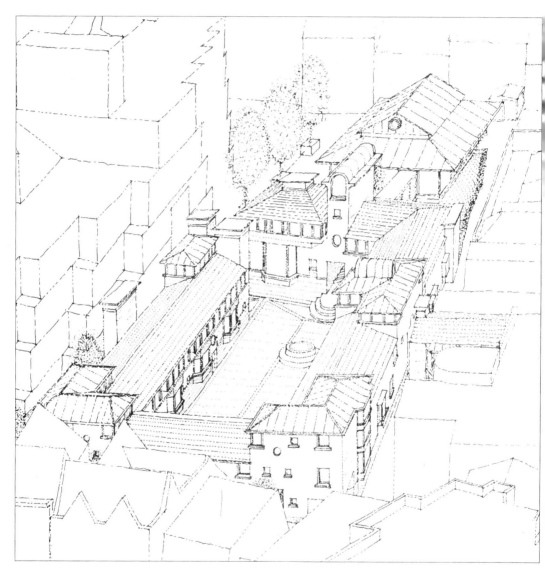

Figure 4.13. Blue Boar Court, Trinity College, Cambridge. MacCormac Jamieson Prichard. (a) The accommodation is broken down into small-scale parts to fit into the space between the existing tall buildings.

Figure 4.13. (b) Courtyard view (photograph Peter Cook)

and articles in the press. This design attitude obviously needs to be included in this chapter, but in a somewhat cautionary way; not because it is not a useful criterion, but because it is fraught with pitfalls and needs to be handled carefully. It should not be assumed, for example, that the use of local materials and scale of development will automatically produce good architecture, especially good modern architecture. There are several design factors involved.

This approach is too often used as a sort of medicine: the design is indifferent so the facing elevation is clad with local brick and an area of clay tiles is added to the roof. This insipid use of neo-vernacular construction is not good enough. Insistence that local materials and construction have to be used should not be seen as a restriction and automatic route to pastiche design (see section 7.5, 'Building history'). Poor retrospective buildings are blamed, sometimes unfairly, on the demands of the Planning Officer, rather than on the inability of the design team. It is possible to make generative use of local materials and traditions. First, it is necessary to establish exactly what it is that gives the area its distinctiveness.

It should first be noted that the way we now build is less controlled by regional materials and techniques. Modern systems of transport allow economic access to a wide pallet of materials, and construction is now influenced more by management techniques than by local know-how. Similarly, design, including the philosophy of conservation, is now subject to magazines and international debate. None the less, regional identity is still evident, and the older the buildings and the more there are of them, so the evidence remains stronger.

The influence of regional materials and techniques may have diminished in modern construction, and it would be nostalgic to stop this trend, but the influence of climate and geology remains as strong as ever. It is interesting to observe that the increased need for human comfort within buildings has moved architecture to respond to this regional variation of climate and terrain; roofs sweep against the prevailing wind; window size and position reflect site conditions and alignment; the external envelope takes on a mechanistic appearance as large louvres track backwards and forwards following the path of the sun. This type of regional response should be encouraged as it assists the idea of new architecture being apt and appropriate rather than stylish. Renzo Piano demonstrates such an approach through the Menil Arts Gallery, Houston, which protects the valuable exhibits with large expressed louvres curved to counter the harsh Texan sun. Similarly, there is the work of the Parisian architect Jean Nouvel, who uses facades made up of moving parts which are able to moderate the changes in the external environment. The elevations of the Hôtel Saint-James, Bordeaux-Bouliac, are made up of large, hydraulically operated, hinged metal grids which give what Nouvel describes as variable 'fractal vision'. And the leading-edge technology of the metal frames and filters of the Institut du Monde Arabe, Paris, give it an appearance like the iris diaphragm of a camera.[15]

Although regionality is primarily caused by geological or climatic forces, it is in the direct effect of these that the distinctiveness touches the human response. It is often felt through an accumulation of specifics: cobbles, corrie, croft, crux, drystone walls, groynes, hopfields, holm oak, long barrow, moor, millstone grit,

Figure 4.14. Visitors' Centre, Jedburgh Abbey, Scotland. Historic Scotland. A modern design which makes use of traditional construction. (photograph Historic Scotland)

maltings, oast houses, orchards, pit tips, sunken lane, tow path, undulation, weather board, wind, and wold.[16] The designer needs to be able to abstract ideas from these during the evolution of the project.

The problem is that many of these local features and characteristics trigger particular associations to the observer. The danger to the designer is that to merely copy them will be perceived as an assimilation and a pastiche of the original. It takes skill to extract elements of local tradition and use these in a new form of assembly.

The Jedburgh Abbey Visitors' Centre, by Historic Scotland (Fig. 4.14), is obviously modern but makes use of local materials and construction.

Edward Cullinan has gained a reputation for use of traditional materials in modern design. This is seen in his innovative replacement timber roof at St Mary's Church, Barnes, and particularly in the modern Visitors' Centre for Fountains Abbey (Fig. 4.15).

Figure 4.15. Visitors' Centre, Fountains Abbey, Yorkshire. Edward Cullinan's scheme uses traditional materials for a modern design planned to enhance the route to the monument. (photograph Martin Charles)

5

At the monument

This chapter identifies design concepts that assist the integration of new architecture into the fabric of a historic building. It considers ideas which operate at, and within, the actual fabric of the monument. It considers how the design of the new architecture can be generated from factors within the existing fabric.

5.1 The paths of lords and servants

The way we approach a building, enter it, and move through it, can influence our perception and enjoyment of the building and its history. It particularly affects our understanding of the arrangement of the rooms and spaces inside the building. It therefore influences our recognition of the architectural and social hierarchy of the building.

Consider, for example, the footsteps of the lord of the manor and those of a servants' of the estate. The lord approaches the building along a grand driveway: the entrance is evident and imposing and leads into a formal reception space from which a series of rooms is arranged and graded according to protocol. The servant passes along a side track, past the laundry and the back of the brew house to reach a minor door which leads into a confusion of service corridors, servants' rooms, and stores. Charles, in Evelyn Waugh's novel *Brideshead Revisited* (Waugh 1945), is taken by Sebastian into the large house:

> We drove round the front into a side court . . . and entered through the stone-flagged, stone-vaulted passages of the servants' quarters – 'I want you to meet Nanny Hawkins. That's what we've come for' – and climbed uncarpeted, scrubbed elm stairs, followed more passages of wide boards covered in the centre by a thin strip of drugget, through passages covered by linoleum, passing the wells of many minor staircases and many rows of crimson and gold fire buckets, up a final staircase, gated at the head. The dome was false, designed to be seen from below like the cupolas of Chambord. Its drum was merely an additional storey full of segmented rooms. Here were the nurseries.[1]

Each house has a hierarchy, the rooms have a natural gradation. Any change made to the building has to be carried out in such a way that it does not affect our understanding of this arrangement. Architectural intervention into this hierarchical sequence is difficult and can, if not carried out thoughtfully, be detrimental to the integrity of the building. Consider, for example, minor alterations frequently made to a historic house to allow visitors to tour round the rooms. These adjustments, for security, convenience, or privacy, may be minimal in terms of changes to the actual fabric, but the impact, in terms of our understanding and enjoyment of the a building, could be considerable. Blocked doorways and roped-off corridors force visitors to pass along a route that enters round the back of the building, into the servants' rooms, passes across the corner of an imposing reception room, turns into the kitchen, into the library, and then out through the conservatory. Visitors are unable to pass through the sequence of rooms in any meaningful way; they are naturally confused, unable to understand and enjoy the architecture and history of the building.

It is recognised that the social strata of modern society are different from the past; however, it is this which created the specific hierarchy of rooms to form part of the history of the building. Designers have to be aware of this hierarchical matrix to ensure that any new architectural intervention into the building preserves our understanding of the history of the building.

The hierarchical gradation of rooms in the plan of the historic house is reflected in the different types of building construction used for the different parts of the building. It was, for example, natural for the smaller, more cellular parts of the building to be built with traditional timber joisted floors, whereas the larger reception rooms needed more expensive, deep composite beams to span over the wide areas. The building, therefore, takes on a natural morphology; from large volumes to smaller volumes, from deep construction to simple construction (see section 6.2, 'Morphology'). An addition to a historic building needs to reflect, or acknowledge in some form, the grain and construction inherent within each of its particular parts.

Design solutions can respond in several ways. Consider first the way we approach a building. An example of an architectural intervention that helps us to enjoy a direct and dignified approach to a historic building is seen at Hampton Court Palace. Here the Visitors' Centre for tickets, information, and books, has been repositioned; taken out of Base Court and relocated as a modern design within the military stables. This allows the visitor to obtain a ticket and information as part of a natural route up to the main West Front, which then leads through to the series of courts which make up the palace.

The approach to a building has often been specifically designed, a route full of 'pomp and circumstance' or an 'enchanted meander'. Horace Walpole must have spent many pleasant hours dreaming up the entrance into Strawberry Hill; through a small Gothic door, past a secret garden, by a monastic cloister, and into a small hall where you again have to change direction and aspect.

It is generally easier to explain the internal layout of a building via a circulation route that starts at the main entrance. This works well at Kenwood House, Hampstead, where the insertion of a small new control desk within the entrance salon is all that is necessary to supervise the visitors. It is questionable that the new control desk is detailed as a Georgian piece of furniture. It is also a shame that you are then directed sideways out of the corner of the hall rather than forward through the natural hierarchy of rooms.

The intervention can, however, be more substantial; and it is interesting to observe that this more radical approach is more common abroad than in Britain (see section 2.2, 'Present attitudes'). Formation of the Parma Museum, Italy, was only made possible by a confident architectural intervention by Guido Canali. The solution involved forming a new route through the existing group of buildings (Fig. 5.1). This route is designed as a modern lightweight construction, as delicate bridges hung from the structure and thin ramps across the changes of level join together the various spaces into one linear museum.

The Guggenheim Museum in New York has a very specific route through it in the form of the spiralling ramp which creates the gallery space. This is the central idea of Frank Lloyd Wright's building, and it is this spiral of space which gives the Guggenheim its distinctive form. New Yorkers were at first appalled with this strange shape when it opened in 1959 but soon came to regard it with affection. The new tower block extension alongside Wright's building fails to recognise the central theme of the rotunda. It subjugates Wright's spiral to an access way serving the new gallery tower. The scheme by Gwathmey, Siegel, and Associates has caused an equal storm of protest from New Yorkers. The new tower reduces the rotunda from a monument in its own right into what has been dubbed 'a lavatory bowl next to a cistern' (see section 6.3, 'Mother and child').[2]

And finally for this section, an example of urban planning. Lawrence Nield and Partners' scheme[3] for modernising the Passenger Terminal Building, Sydney, involved changing the whole road access pattern so as to create a new pedestrian Rocks Place in this old area of the city overlooking the harbour (Fig. 5.2). The alteration of the existing building is also interesting for the way that it is shortened by a design process of progressively stripping down the layers of construction to its bare skeleton to increase its lightness and transparency;[4] a device used previously by Carlo Scarpa at Castelvecchio, Verona.

5.2 Perceptual transparency

When we look at the external appearance of a building, we are usually able to establish a reasonable idea about the inside of the building: the outside informs us about the interior. The observer picks up this information in three ways. First, by physically looking into the building through the windows or doors. Second, through an understanding of the significance of the plan, general shape, massing,

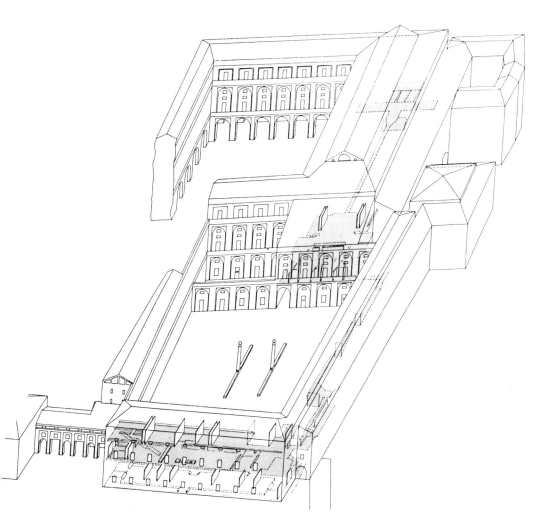

Figure 5.1. Museum of Art, Palazzo della Pilotta, Parma, Italy. Guido Canali. Modern lightweight construction is used to form a new circulation route through the various parts of the palazzo. (reproduced from *Architectural Review*)

and the size and arrangement of the windows: we recognise, for example, that a series of closely grouped large windows probably encloses a large space, and we can imagine what sort of internal volumes are enclosed by the shape of the external fabric. And third, through an understanding of the building's iconographic symbols: do these tell us that it is a 'type of castle', or a particular 'type of church', or a regional 'type of house'? We know from experience that each of these 'types' has its own recognisable arrangement, and our knowledge of the tradition of each type leads us to expect, to anticipate, a particular interior.

Examples of the first method, that is the physical act of looking into the interior through glass, can produce some exciting schemes. The new glass wall in front of the Palau de la Música Catalana, Barcelona (Fig. 5.3) provides new foyer space for a modern staircase up to the auditorium. Oscar Tusquets, Lluís Clotet and Carlos Diaz have designed this sheer and minimalist glazing as a transparent screen in front of Lluís Domenech's turn-of-the-century building; the exuberant details of the existing building can, therefore, be seen clearly from the urban square through the new foyer (see section 5.3, 'Inside or outside space').[5] The support for the glazing is calm and less obtrusive than the mass of tensile rods seen at many modern glass wall structures. The result gets close to Walter Gropius's ambition for a 'dematerialization of the enclosing structure'.[6]

The second and third approaches to transparency present a dilemma. The ideas of transparency through building shape and its symbolic references are in themselves straightforward. However, the question arises in terms of conservation, does this matter? The question can be addressed by looking at two different buildings. For example, at Marble Hill, Twickenham (a straightforward Palladian-type villa) the observer is able to visualise the sort of interior behind the facade. However, at the theatre in Richmond, Yorkshire, the visitor will be proved wrong; the external facade suggests a small warehouse, but a surprise awaits inside in the form of a charming little Georgian auditorium. This interior is a sort of artificial world, a stage set constructed within the shell of the building.

It is up to the designer to know what game is being played, what the original architect was trying to achieve. Does the historic interior belong naturally to the outside appearance of the building or is it a 'theatrical insert'? We are reminded of Immanuel Kant's observations that we see more than the image received by our eyes: we understand more than we actually see. When we look at a table we see two or three legs but we understand that the table has four.

Colin Rowe explores the idea of perceptual transparency in the important essay 'Literal and phenomena transparency'[7] This is a complex text with a density of terminology. It does little justice to summarise his observations but, in general terms, he divides the subject into 'literal transparency', by which he refers to the physical act of a material transmitting light, and 'phenomena transparency', which is then subdivided into 'apparent', as in a perspective drawing of space, and 'abstract', as in the uncertain impression of space portrayed through a Braque painting.[8]

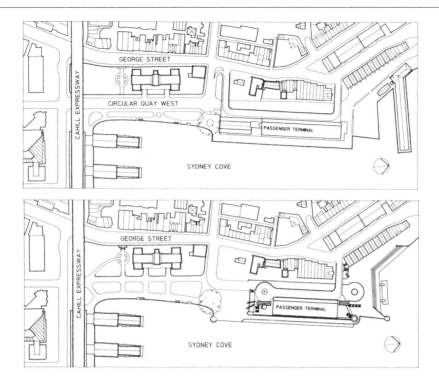

Figure 5.2. Ocean Terminal Building, Sydney. Lawrence Nield and Partners. (a) The road access is revised to form the pedestrian Rocks Place. (b) Exterior view. (plans and photograph courtesy of Lawrence Nield and Partners)

The idea of phenomena transparency leads on to the argument for or against the retention of the front facades of historic buildings. This town planning device of preserving the historic appearance of an area while allowing the redevelopment of the site behind it has become popular in the last decade. It has been seen by developers as a way to appease planning control. Examples are numerous, such as the internal redevelopment of St Paul's House, Leeds, or 118–120 Colmore Row, Birmingham.[9]

This is taken further with some developments which actually rebuild the front facade. The 'Victorian' frontage of the Grand Buildings site at Trafalgar Square, London, for example, is completely new, built with modern construction to wrap around a new open-plan office interior. The new facade by Ron Sidell and Paul Gibson fortunately makes improvements on the 1896 building by F. and H. Francis, particularly in the introduction of a ground-level arcade which makes it more welcoming to the square.[10] This scheme should present a teaser for future historians.

The problem with many of these new developments behind historic facades is that the window pattern of the original building usually portrays a tight grain of small cellular internal rooms whereas the actual new interior is made up of those new, large, open-plan volumes now required by commercial clients.

Your position in the debate depends on how you see the facade; either as a superficial understanding of the whole site being historic, or as a flat stage set which gives no more than a superficial appearance of a historic building.

There are, however, adjustments in the way we look at the problem, different ways of perceiving the facade. What happens if we perceive the facade as a skin? The skin of an orange or a coconut are not the same as their interior: is it right that we should expect the interior of a solid to look the same as its outside? Anish Kapoor's winning submission for the 1991 Turner Art Prize stimulates the sense of surprise in looking into a solid; his giant natural stones are carved out with unexpected secretive and brightly coloured interiors which undermine the solidity of the exterior.[11] The problem with architecture is that we have evolved an expectation that the exterior is a natural expression of what is going on inside. There are, of course, exceptions, but these do not alter our general understanding. Retained facades in front of new interiors break down this biological analogy, the skin and the interior are of different periods in time.

This difference can, however, be exploited. If, for example, the identities of the two ages are separately stated, then a dialogue can be set up between the new and the old. The pretence is removed, the observer is no longer confused. The original stone arch entrance to the old Lloyds Building, London, was retained to stand in front of, but visually separate from, Richard Rogers's modern structure. Each strengthens the difference of the other, like Anish Kapoor's sculpture, there is a mental tension between the exterior view and that which is covered.

An interesting variant is the new office block at Knowle Green, Walton-on-Thames, by Nicholas Hare (Fig. 5.4). The planning requirement for a traditional brick facade is fulfilled, and at the same time 'used', to create a free-

Figure 5.3. Palau de la Música Catalana, Barcelona. Oscar Tusquets, Lluís Clotet and Carlos Diaz. A new glass front encloses space for a new staircase to the auditorium. (photograph Hisao Suzuki)

standing visual screen in front of the modern office building: it acts as both a 'historic' and an 'environmental' filter.

Roger Stephenson's restoration of Trinity Court, Dalton Street, Manchester, makes deliberate emphasis on the idea of the interior coming through the historic facade in order to provide a hint, or a clue, as to the nature of the interior design. The new entrance canopy (Fig. 5.5) is placed and detailed to demonstrate the modern interior. Stephenson, together with Simpson Associates, was the subject of an exhibition at The Royal Institute of British Architects in 1992.[12] Their work portrays an alternative approach to new architecture in an old context. By using an architectural language that fulfils today's needs, they adopt the city's spirit without plagiarising the past; they express confidence in the future, whilst allowing the past to retain its dignity.

This idea of layering of the fabric is exploited by Carlo Scarpa in his restoration and conversion of Castelvecchio, Verona, into the City Museum.[13] He makes clear definition and visual separation of the new wall and floor surfaces, while at the end of the galleries, where he inserts a new staircase, he pulls back the fabric of the historic building by peeling back one layer at a time. The effect is both informative and sculpturally pleasing.

At Biržų Street, Vilnius, the restoration by Jonas Glemža and Romanas Jaloveckas retains the evidence of previous times in the form of the marks of the previous buildings as a conscious component of the elevation (Fig. 5.6).[14]

Richard Bryant's celebrated photograph of the glass envelope of Norman Foster's Willis Faber Dumas Office, Ipswich, illustrates an elevation that uses transient reflections of history. An idea used also by Manser Associates in 1973 for a new reflective glass building placed alongside the eighteenth-century Thorncroft Manor, Surrey, so as to capture its reflections in the new facade.[15]

5.3 Inside or outside space

Architectural intervention at a historical site is often the key to unlock a new future for the buildings. This section considers schemes where the intervention has been used to transform an existing external space into new, usable, internal accommodation. In doing so, it has provided an alternative way to use the building, it has provided additional accommodation or unlocked a new circulation route to allow new ways through the building.

The first example encloses the open space of a street in Leeds to form a shopping mall. Derek Latham's glass roof between the buildings forms the new pedestrian area to give life and a sense of place to the street (Fig. 5.7). A new roof over the back area between two office blocks in Store Street, London, was similarly used to join the two buildings together. Here (Fig. 5.8) a new centre is formed in the old courtyard for the Imagination Building. Herron Associates use a modern,

Figure 5.4. Offices, Knowle Green, Walton-on-Thames. Nicholas Hare. A traditional brick elevation is used as a 'filter' in front of the modern glazing to overcome both town planning and environmental restraints. (photograph Martin Green)

Figure 5.5. Trinity Court, Dalton Street, Manchester. Roger Stephenson allows the modern interior to be seen externally by projecting it through the historic facade. (drawing Roger Stephenson)

PVC-coated polyester scrim fabric roof and lightweight metal bridges and decks to create a new modern focus. Note that the elevations of the existing buildings are left as they were; window sills and wall surfaces still portray the idea of outside space.

Large courtyards can be transformed with new roofs into usable accommodation. This has been achieved with a neat pyramidical glass roof over the square courtyard of the old Hospital de San Rafael, Santander, Spain. The new roof, and thus the new use of the courtyard, was the key to conversion of the unused hospital into a seat for local government.[16]

The Imperial War Museum, London, is also housed in a former hospital.[17] The museum was established in the buildings in 1920. In 1983 Arup Associates were appointed to prepare a feasibility study for the phased redevelopment of the museum. An important part of this programme was roofing over the main courtyard (Fig. 5.9). The non-directional arrangement of the structural members and the controlled detailing of the new glass give an appropriate feeling of 'sky' to the roof over the suspended aeroplanes.

The New York International Design Centre has been formed within a row of four, early twentieth-century concrete factories. Here the space of the open court of the Centre 1 building has been enclosed within a glass vault to form an exhibition space (Fig. 5.10). A large staircase is added into the new space to link the floors together.

This same approach can be used at a smaller scale, at a size appropriate to many historic buildings. At the Royal Society of Arts, John Adam Street, London, the external space at the rear of the buildings has been enclosed for a new staircase linking the sub-basement vaults with the upper floors. The vaults, previously isolated and used by a wine merchant, now provide lecture, exhibition, and restaurant space as part of the regular activities of the RSA. The new enclosed area and the new staircase have been carefully crafted by Green Lloyd Architects to retain the identity of the original buildings (Fig. 5.11). The use of bleached oak, exposed steelwork, and York stone paving retains the atmosphere of an external courtyard. The external walls of the existing building are retained as 'external' walls, unplastered and untreated with 'internal'-type decoration. This ability to retain the sense of external place helps visitors to know where they are in relationship to the existing buildings (see also Sackler Galleries, Fig. 8.3).

5.4 Enclosures

The previous section considered the idea of enclosing external space to produce a new way of using a historic building. This section also looks at the idea of enclosing space, but here the purpose is to enclose the actual fabric of the historic site with the aim of protecting it from further deterioration.

The inquisitive urge to find factual evidence about the past is necessary in any

Figure 5.6. Biržų Street, Vilnius. Jonas Glemža and Romanas Jaloveckas. The restoration retains the marks of previous buildings. (reproduced from *Monumentum*, March 1984)

society: nevertheless, archaeological digs have to be considered very carefully before work begins. One important question has to be addressed, namely what will happen to the unearthed and exposed fabric after the archaeologists have left the site? What will need to be done to exhibit it? And, of particular importance to this study, what will need to be done to protect it?

A common solution is to construct a protective enclosure over the remains. What are the design parameters for these structures? The excavated finds are often very fragile, the firm outer layer of ashlar stone has often been stolen in the past so that what we now discover is only the soft, inner rubble core of the old walls. And decorative floor pavings are now exposed to face the rain clouds rather than the original ceilings. These remains are invariably porous, requiring some type of enclosure to keep off the rain. The problem is that this waterproof enclosure can simultaneously induce a micro-climate inside the enclosure to cause more damage than the rain: the warm, dry, internal atmosphere draws moisture out of the ground up into the porous and fragile stonework, and this wet and dry sequence soon breaks down the stone. It is, therefore, necessary to produce an enclosure that maintains a suitable and stable internal environment.

The first example is the site of the Roman Military Baths, Caerleon, Gwent (Fig. 5.12). The correct humidity is maintained by moisture jets beneath the raised walkways. The interior of this protective building, with so many walkways and bridges, shows the dilemma of new architecture getting in the way of seeing what is being protected.

An alternative approach is to allow natural ventilation through the new enclosure. This is provided in the protective cover for Sueno's Stone, Forres, Moray, by Historic Scotland (Fig. 5.13). The louvres top and bottom induce a through-draught to prevent condensation on the stone and on the enclosing glass. The metal columns appear heavy for the size of the structure.

These enclosures present a problem for the designer; what should the new building look like? The new structure has to be larger and positioned over the top of the fragile fabric. The new architecture could well be intrusive, detract from interest in the historical remains, get in the way. The observer could find the new architecture more interesting than the history. It is necessary to generate the design of the new building from the historic remains, but to do so in a restrained way – using, for example, repetition of the plan shapes of the building rather than playful metaphor. The new architecture needs to be seen to belong to the site. It should be simple, carefully edited in its detailing, and well crafted.

Simplicity is demonstrated in Peter Zumthor's work in Switzerland. The remains of three Roman houses at Chur are protected with elegant ventilated sheds. Here the ventilation uses the principle of an agricultural 'Dutch barn'. Zumthor uses his carpentry experience and his time working on historic buildings to create a series of modern timber boxes which follow the geometry of the houses and allow the breeze and dim warm light to enter through the louvre-like slats of the enclosing walls.[18]

Figure 5.7. Shopping mall, Victoria Quarter, Leeds. Derek Latham. The street is enclosed with a new glazed canopy. Decorative glass by Brian Clarke. (photograph Stuart Blackwood)

5.5 New roofs and umbrellas

An alternative method of forming a protective micro-climate around the fragile remains is to construct a protective roof in the form of an umbrella.

An example is at Witney, near Oxford, where a lightweight, teflon-coated, canvas umbrella has been constructed over the exposed remains of the twelfth-century Bishop's Palace (Fig. 5.14). This approach avoids the build-up of an adverse closed environment but does present the problem of getting the new umbrella at just the right height to keep the archaeological remains dry and frost-free. It is difficult to predict exactly how it is going to work throughout the seasonal variations and some sort of adjustment should be built in.

A similar approach is used by the United States National Parks Service for a cover over the remains of the tenth-century houses of the Basket Weaver Community of New Mexico (Fig. 5.15). Here, the protection is a solid flat roof of laminated timber beams supporting a space frame, and canvas screens are added around the edge in response to changes in the weather.

We now see sophisticated facades to our modern buildings with large louvres which automatically track backwards and forwards with the sun, and external elevations made up of several layers of glass, sun-shaded walkways, warm air voids, and adjustable ventilators. All of this generates a new architectural language which will no doubt be used some time in the future as a natural and appropriate protection to our historic remains (see section 4.7, 'Regional traditions' – the work of Renzo Piano and Jean Nouvel).

Modern umbrellas can also be formed over larger remains, used as a replacement for historic roofs lost at some time in the past. The problem at Rochester Castle, Kent, of dampness and bird lime causing damage to the fine Norman stone carvings within the interior has led to the proposal to construct a new glass roof over the shell of the keep (Fig. 5.16). The modern roof, designed by Manning and Clamp, will not only protect the interior but also allow for a more suitable use and presentation of the enclosed space.

The designer has to decide if the new protective cover is located in a plane over the top of the remains or in the plane of the original roof. Each needs a different approach to the way it is detailed. The umbrella should avoid any reference to the lost roof, and the gap between the top of the remains and the umbrella should be clearly expressed in order to accentuate the idea of a new cover floating over the top of the ruin. A new cover in the plane of the original roof could well take reference from the rhythm of the old lead roof rolls or the shape of a special ridge feature; nevertheless, it should be clear that the new cover is a piece of new architecture and not a replica of the original.

The question of alignment of the new protective cover is seen at the Blackfriars site at Gloucester. The protective cover here is not a roof but it does illustrate the point. The dark glass screen wall inserted to enclose the nave cuts across the line of the south transept and thus changes the perceived shape of the original

Figure 5.8. The Imagination Building, Store Street, London. Herron Associates. The space between the rear of two buildings is enclosed with a modern tent roof, with new bridges and a staircase to link the accommodation. (photograph Martin Charles)

monument (Fig. 5.17). Although it is neatly detailed, it gives a confused and inaccurate idea about the monastic church to the visitor.

The new roof at the Schloss, Gottesaue, Karlsruhe, falls into this ambiguous world between new architecture and restoration. The palace has been restored from a ruined shell to form a new music centre. The criterion was adopted that the exterior should resemble the original. However, within this framework, the architects Staatliches Hochbauamt I Karlsruhe have designed modern detailing for the fenestration and have 'recalled' the large lead ridge of the original roof as a key for the design of a new linear roof light which permits the roof space to be used as new modern accommodation.[19]

Hans Döllgast's pioneering work in the early use of modern architecture for the conservation of historic buildings was discussed in Chapter 2 (see section 2.1, 'Views of history'). His work also included two excellent modern roof structures over churches that had lost their roofs during the Second World War. St Bonifaz, and Allerheiligenhof, both in Munich (Fig. 5.18), are given modern, lightweight timber roofs formed using lots of tensile members and a shape which implies sympathy with, yet separation from, the remains of the historic church.

5.6 Egg in the basket

It is possible for one building to sit inside a larger building; that is, for it to appear to be sitting inside another building. Consider the larger building (that is the basket) to be a large Victorian building, and the smaller (that is the egg) to be something small and overtly modern placed within the Victorian interior. The two parts are perceived to be different, they are perceived to be of different types of construction, of different styles, built in different ages. Each has its own identity. That is not to say that the new modern design statement should not have some form of empathy with the Victorian interior, some sort of design reference or association.

A direct example is the Royal Exchange Theatre in Manchester, designed by Levitt Bernstein in the 1970s (Fig. 5.19).[20] Here a modern steel skeleton frame structure forms the new 'theatre module' which sits under the central dome of the nineteenth-century Exchange Building. The new theatre and the old exchange room retain their separate identity. This is a useful design device to allow for a new, or additional, way of using the historic building without losing the identity of the original building. This approach was used by Richard Rogers in inserting the new trading floor for the conversion of Billingsgate Fish Market into a building for modern finance.

The same characteristics are frequently seen at large railway stations. The timber pavilions at Glasgow Central appear as individual small pavilions within the volume beneath the impressive Edwardian girders of the main concourse. Similarly, the neatly detailed glass enclosure for the Information Centre at Newcastle Station appears as a separate modern glass box beneath the larger space of the station shed.

Figure 5.9. Imperial War Museum, Lambeth, London. Arup Associates, Architects + Engineers + Quantity Surveyors. The courtyard is enclosed with a new glass vault to form a large exhibition space. (drawing Arup Associates)

Two neatly crafted examples from Dublin. The first is new accommodation inserted into existing buildings at Trinity College by De Blacam and Meagher (Fig. 5.20). The space was created following fire damage in the Dining Hall and Kitchens. The new atrium is used for circulation and also as a drama studio: note the first-floor shutters which allow alternative degrees of privacy from the landing corridors. The second example is at a domestic scale, where Cochrane Flynn-Rogers and Williams have formed a small, self-contained flat within the *piano nobile* of a large Georgian terraced house in North Great Georges Street. This retains the size and elegance of the principal room and creates an octagonal *trompe-l'oeil* 'garden' enclosure in the centre of the smaller front room to form a dining space and conceal the kitchenette, bathroom, and stores within the corners. The architectural insertion, with its painted stone walls and hedges, is detailed to sit as an egg in the basket of the Georgian room, never apparently touching the existing fabric.

The designer of this type of insertion has to appreciate the original and the new as separate objects, the architectural details of each will then become clear and the observer will be able to appreciate the value of both. Green Lloyd's new access stair for the formation of the new Witt Library in the basement of Somerset House does just this (Fig. 5.21). There is plenty of space around the new staircase to allow it to be perceived separately, it can be seen in the round like looking at a piece of sculpture.

Conversion of the Amsterdam Stock Exchange into a series of concert spaces was made possible by the insertion of a new glass auditorium within the AGA hall (Fig. 5.22). The distinctive details of Hendrik Petrus Berlage's exchange of 1898–1903 are shown to their full in, and through the glass of Pieter Zaanen's new acoustic envelope with its slow curving 'cello' belly.

And finally, there is a charming example at Osborne House on the Isle of Wight, where Queen Victoria had a glass conservatory built within the first-floor colonnade to enable her to walk into the adjoining wing without getting cold.[21] The new glass link, built in 1850, stands within the structure of the colonnade like a small doll's house.

5.7 A sense of separation

The significance of the space between the new architecture and the existing fabric is developed in this section. The issue here is for the designer to achieve a sense of separation between the new and the original. The reason for this is to make a clear statement, and thus establish a clear understanding, of what is new and what is historic.

At the Legionary Museum, Caerleon, Wales, a dark glass screen is used to form the separation between the existing museum and the new extension (Fig. 5.23). It creates a negative recess between the two parts.

The significance of the blank recess is often underestimated; its role in the design

Figure 5.10. New York International Design Centre, Long Island City, USA. Master plan I. M. Pei, architect Gwathmey Siegel and Associates. The open court of the concrete factory is utilised by a new staircase and glazed roof; the interior is enhanced with modern fixtures and graphics. (photograph Richard Bryant/Arcaid)

process little considered. The recess, gap, separator, call it what you will, is used in other forms of art. Its role in music, in the form of a silent pause, is interesting. Consider, for example, the opening of Beethoven's Fifth, or Wagner, in the Prelude to Tristan and Isolde. The pause allows separation between the phrases. The moment of silence allows contemplation of the phrase, yet, at the same time, awaits, in anticipation, the next musical statement. The pause stimulates thought both backwards and forwards.[22]

In architecture the gap also assists in the appreciation of the adjoining statements. It should not be considered as an architectural subordinate but as a contemplatory counterpoint.

The separation does not have to be actual or a glass link, it can be implied. The Combination Room added to Downing College, Cambridge, in 1970, achieves this sense of implied separation (Fig. 5.24). The design, by Howell Killick Partridge and Amis, uses a length of blank stone wall to achieve the separation between the portico of William Wilkins's original neo-classical buildings[23] and the modern classicism of the new combination room. The separating wall is pushed back so that it appears less important, thus leaving the two classical elements as strong separate statements. The wall, that is the connector, becomes a negative recess, albeit with accommodation behind to provide service rooms and a link between new and old.

This sense of separation can also be used to advantage in the design of smaller architectural interventions. The new staircase in the Monastery Père de Roda, Spain, has been raised slightly over the remains of the original so that the gap beneath the new structure helps to give the impression of the new architecture floating over the original; there is no confusion as to what is new and what is old. The same approach was used by John Winter for the new metal staircase leading up to the entrance of Rochester Castle in Kent.

Figure 5.11. Royal Society of Arts, John Adam Street, London. Green Lloyd Architects. External space is enclosed for a new staircase to link the vaults with the upper floors; the existing elevations retain the appearance of 'external' walls. (photograph Jo Reid and John Peck)

Figure 5.12. Roman Military Baths, Caerleon, Gwent. Welsh Historic Monuments. The building forms an environmentally controlled enclosure over the Roman remains; humidifiers are located under the walkways. (photograph James Strike)

Figure 5.13. Sueno's Stone, Forres, Morayshire. Historic Scotland. A glass cover incorporating permanent ventilation to reduce the build-up of heat. (photograph Historic Scotland)

Figure 5.14. Site of the Bishop's Palace, Witney, Oxford. English Heritage. A protective canvas cover to protect the stone remains from the rain and frost damage. (photograph Nick Reading)

Figure 5.15. Site of the Basket Weaver houses, New Mexico, USA. A protective roof over the remains; canvas awnings are added around the side walls in winter. (photograph John Fidler)

Figure 5.16. Rochester Castle, Kent. Manning Clamp and Partners. A proposed glass roof over the castle keep to protect the Norman stonework and to allow a more informative interpretation within the new interior. (drawing Manning Clamp and Partners)

Figure 5.17. Blackfriars, Gloucester. English Heritage. The new glass wall cuts across the south transept rather than reforming the line of the original monastic church plan. (photograph James Strike)

Figure 5.18. St Bonifaz, Munich. Hans Döllgast. A modern lightweight timber roof delicately placed over the war-damaged church. (Architektur Museum Technischen, Universität München)

Figure 5.19. Royal Exchange Theatre, Manchester. Concept by Richard Negri, architects Levitt Bernstein Associates. The new theatre, constructed in 1975, sits as a separate design statement within the existing building, Bradshaw Gass and Hope, 1874. (photograph Anthony Weller)

90

Figure 5.20. Trinity College, Dublin. De Blacam and Meagher. A new atrium and drama space inserted within the shell of the building after fire damage. (photograph Richard Linzey)

91

Figure 5.21. The Witt Library, Somerset House, London. Green Lloyd Architects' new communi
cation staircase stands like a 'piece of modern sculpture' within the historic interior. (photograph J
Reid and John Peck)

Figure 5.22. Stock Exchange Building, Amsterdam. Pieter Zaanen. A new glass auditorium constructed within the existing building, Hendrik Berlage, 1898–1903. (photograph Richard Bryant/Arcaid)

Figure 5.23. Legionary Museum, Caerleon, Wales. Welsh Historic Monuments. A dark glass screen is used to form a visual separation between the existing museum and the new extension. (photograph James Strike)

Figure 5.24. Combination Room, Downing College, Cambridge. 1965–70, Howell Killick Partridge and Amis. The blank stone wall forms a visual separation between the existing and the new classical statements. (photograph Brecht Einzig)

6

Connections by assimilation

This chapter considers the process by which new architecture can be linked to a historic site by forming a reference to a physical element of the existing historic fabric. That is, the design for the new architecture is generated by assimilation of an existing element of the site.

The connection relies primarily on the psychology of 'grouping'.[1] We have a natural tendency to group similar things together; we sort out the books in the bookcase, and we make neat assumptions about similar people. We can make use of this tendency of 'grouping' to link the new architecture to the historic fabric.

The link between the new architecture and the historical site does not have to be a physical connection, nor is it necessary for it to be a direct replication of the existing fabric; it will work better if the connection acts at a more mental, rather than physical, level; it needs to achieve an intellectual link.

6.1 Shape and proportion

Assimilation can work in several ways, the design reference can be made to different aspects of the historic fabric: it is like arranging the books in the bookcase by different systems of classification.

One of the easiest forms to recognise is a design reference made to the basic shapes found in the historic fabric. A simple and explanatory example is the design of the Tiltyard restaurant at Hampton Court Palace, where the new canopy takes its reference from the shape of the crenellations of the Tudor tower (Fig. 6.1). The new architecture is referential to, rather than an exact copy of, the original fabric.

Assimilation can also be made with the geometry of the historic site. An interesting example is Bernhard Blauel's extension of a villa in Abraham Lincoln Strasse, Weimar. Blauel takes the existing geometry of interlocking rectangles of the existing plan and extends this both horizontally and vertically to form the new accommodation (Fig. 6.2).

Figure 6.1. The Tiltyard Restaurant, Hampton Court Palace, London. Department of the Environment. The new roof takes its shape from the crenellations of the tower.

Figure 6.2. Villa in Abraham Lincoln Strasse, Weimar. Bernhard Blauel. The new extension reflects in three dimensions the geometry of interlocking rectangles of the existing plan. (photograph Bernard Blauel)

96

Figure 6.3. Christian IV's church hall at Koldinghaus, Denmark. Johannes Exner. The new light fittings replicate the lines of the lost structural cross vaults. (reproduced from *Monumentum*, December 1984)

Michael Hopkins recasts the geometry of the original design of Bracken House in the City of London for its conversion from the old printing house of the *Financial Times* into a modern office block. The original building, completed in 1959, was designed by Sir Albert Richardson based on Guarino Guarini's seventeenth-century Palazzo Carignano in Turin.[2] Hopkins takes out the central section, which housed the outdated printing presses, and inserts a new oval of atrium and office space. Although the new geometry of this insertion is strong, in fact closer to Carignano than Richardson's scheme, the handling of the new oval drum raises questions in its ambivalence between being a dominant or a subservient element between the retained 'book ends' of Richardson's building; and also in the use of seductive glazing derived from Paris at the turn of the century.[3]

Johannes Exner's new light fittings for Christian IV's church hall in the old royal castle of Koldinghaus, Denmark,[4] take their shape from the vaults which used to roof over the space (Fig. 6.3). The assimilation is, therefore, formed with a memory of the historic fabric, a recall of the lost fabric.

Taking further this idea of memory recall generated through assimilation of lost fabric leads to Franklin Court, Philadelphia. This small open space off Market Street is the site of Benjamin Franklin's home, where Venturi and Rauch have now created a museum below ground[5] and a stainless steel open frame to delineate the profile of the lost fabric of Franklin's house (Fig. 6.4). The sculptural frame gives a sense of presence of the house in the open space.

The problem of making an assimilation recall too literal a statement is demonstrated at the site of the reassembled Crystal Palace at Sydenham.[6] A proposed scheme for a new hotel on the site replicates the original shapes of Paxton's building so closely that any sense of mental participation or involvement by the observer is lost: as such, this tends to destroy our memories of the real building.[7]

Assimilation can also be used to form a connection with the location of a historic site. Portchmouth Russum and Birds make use of this for the new car park close by the historic city of Chichester. The problem set by the city council's open architectural competition was to provide car spaces conveniently close to the historic centre. This winning scheme shows how thoughtful modern architecture can overcome the seemingly impossible task of building a multi-storey car park adjacent to a historic city. The new architecture assimilates the existing city wall which is extended both as a screen to the car park and as a safe wall-walk into the city (Fig. 6.5) (see also section 4.5). Access stairs from the new wall-walk to the car decks take the image of towers along a city wall. The scheme is carefully detailed, the design is clearly generated by the existing city wall but is in no way a pastiche copy; the bonding pattern of the new brickwork is set at a diagonal to create the impression of movement along the facade towards the city entrance, and the honeycomb construction provides ventilation to the ground floor of the car park.

An interesting example, although peripheral to the main subject of this book, is Robinson College, Cambridge, where the idea of a 'city wall' is also used in the design process. Gillespie Kydd and Coia make use of the site location to convey

Figure 6.4. Franklin Court, Philadelphia, 1972. Venturi and Rauch use a steel frame to delineate the site and profile of Benjamin Franklin's house. (photograph John Fidler)

99

the impression that the new collegiate accommodation is formed within the cross-sectional width of a boundary wall along the eastern edge of Cambridge.

6.2 Morphology

The word 'morphology' has its roots in biology, it refers to the way the various parts of a body are assembled together and how each interacts with the other. The word has now taken on a more general meaning and it is used here in an architectural sense to refer to the various parts of a building, their relative size, how they are arranged, and how they interact. The concept is explored in D'Arcy Thompson, *Growth and Form* (D'Arcy Thompson 1942), and Christopher Alexander, *Notes on the Synthesis of Form* (Alexander 1964).

Chapter 4 considered how the size of the building, the size of the building plot, and the way these join together, could be used to stimulate an appropriate design for a new piece of architecture. Similarly, the grain and matrix of the actual building at the site, that is, the type and arrangement of its parts, or its 'morphology', can also be used to generate the new architecture. The idea is that the new design can assimilate this grain and matrix formed by the individual parts of the existing building; the designer thus responds to the 'anatomy' and organisation of the existing building.

From this we see that there is a difference between adding to an existing building made up of numerous, small, cellular volumes and adding to a building made up of a single, wide-span large volume.

A design which breaks down the total volume of the new accommodation into a small-scaled morphology is the Benedictine Abbey at Königsmunster, Meschede, Germany (Fig. 6.6). Each of its component parts is expressed separately.

MacCormac Jamieson and Prichard produced a design for a new chapel at Tonbridge School, Kent, which assimilates the structural morphology of the Edwardian Gothic chapel which was destroyed by fire in 1988. Regrettably, the new design was blocked by a group of vociferous objectors in favour of restoring the Gothic revival building.

Respect for existing structural and planning morphology is evident in Shay Cleary's work in the creation of the new Irish Museum of Modern Art within the Royal Hospital, Kilmainham, Dublin (Fig. 6.7). The new entrance and circulation foyer is a clear, crisp insertion into the existing fabric; the dark glazing is tonally unobtrusive between the columns of the courtyard colonnade, and the white columns alongside the new staircase retain the significance of the structural spine wall of the colonnade and first-floor corridor of the dormitory plan.[8]

The exceptionally high columns of the Victorian church in Jewry Street, Winchester, were exploited by Plincke Leaman and Browning in their modern isation of the United Church. The new floor inserted through the volume retains sufficient height of column shaft to provide a conventionally proportioned interior for the new church space (Fig. 6.8). New meeting rooms beneath the

Figure 6.5. The Avenue de Chartres car park, Chichester, Sussex. Portchmouth Russum and Birds. (a) The plan extends the city wall to form a screen for the new car park and a wall-walk into the city. (b) View of the footbridge over the Avenue de Chartres. (plan and photograph courtesy of Portchmouth Russum and Birds)

new floor are neatly planned around the existing columns, and the original school rooms at the rear have been replaced by a new formal round room enclosed within a spiral ramp which gives a welcomed dignity for the disabled.

6.3 Mother and child

There is a special relationship between a mother and her child, a relationship which comes from a sense of belonging, of having been born of the mother. It is probable that the child will look like the mother once grown out of those particular baby features: not identical, but similar in looks and characteristics. We see a similarity in architecture in the relationship between the chapter house and its cathedral.

The analogy is useful but limited in that the child, unlike architecture, continues to grow, develop, and change. Moving the analogy into nature is again useful, albeit restricted. Observe, for example, how some seedlings blossom as grown-up versions of the early form, yet others evolve in such unlikely ways, and it is only our past experience which prepares us for the metamorphosis of the caterpillar into the butterfly. Is there an equivalent in architecture? Is there such a thing as a natural architectural seedling which we would recognise as belonging to the fully grown architectural flower? Again the chapter house to cathedral seems appropriate; or the gate lodge to the manor house. The gate lodge is not a scaled-down replica of the manor but might well indicate the type of house that the visitor will find at the end of the drive. The biological analogy thus moves the designer to consider the existing historic building as being 'progenitive', being capable of producing an offspring.

The extension of the parish church of Knock in Connacht, southern Ireland, is a suitable example to consider this notion. The new glass enclosure follows the rules of assimilation in its repetition of the shape of the gable wall against which locals witnessed the famous apparition of the Virgin in 1879. Nevertheless, the new Chapel of the Apparition fails to portray a sense of being the offspring of the progenitive church (Fig. 6.9). The reason for this is in the relative size of the new against the original, it is too large to be considered as a child of the mother church.

Although the relationship between a mother and child gradually evolves into that of two grown-ups, this idea of equal status does not work in terms of new architecture alongside existing historic buildings. It is important to keep the new in a subservient role. Article 6 of the Venice Charter states:

> The conservation of a monument implies preserving a setting which is not out of scale. . . . No new construction, demolition or modification which would alter the relations of mass and colour must be allowed.

It is the historic element of the site which has to remain dominant with the new intervention kept subordinate.

The proposal to build a two-storey exhibition and conference block on to the

Figure 6.6. Benedictine Abbey, Königsmunster, Meschede, Germany. Professor Kulka. The accommodation is broken down into small-scale building blocks. (photograph Rheinzink GmbH)

Figure 6.7. Irish Museum of Modern Art within the Royal Hospital, Kilmainham, Dublin. Shay Cleary Architects. A new foyer and staircase with the line of columns retaining the significance of the structural spine wall of the first floor dormitory plan. Original building, 1680–6, Sir William Robinson. (photograph Paul Woodfield)

103

Brontës' Parsonage at Haworth, West Yorkshire, falls into this trap (Fig. 6.10). The historic house would be overwhelmed by the size of the new architecture, the Parsonage would appear a mere annexe, and the relationship between the Brontës' family home and the landscape, which features in the sisters' novels, would be altered.[9]

6.4 Transitions

A variation in the use of replication of parts of a historic site to form new architecture is the idea of transition. That is, the historic fabric is at first copied then modified in some way.

A common type of modification is to grade the replication: a particular feature of the existing building can be not only assimilated in the design of the new architecture, but also graded in its intensity, that is, the degree of replication can begin as a strong statement and then gradually fade across the facade of the new building as it moves further away from the historic building. The influence of the original thus becomes transitional. This device is clearly illustrated through Venturi, Scott Brown and Associates' design for the new Sainsbury Wing of the National Gallery in Trafalgar Square (Fig. 6.11). The classical language of Wilkins's National Gallery is adopted as an element to assimilate in the new architecture. The Corinthian order is copied in its full richness for the cluster of columns nearest to the existing classical frontage. The order is then graded down as it re-occurs across the new gallery; the column spacing increases, the dentils go, and the string courses disappear so that the facade gradually quietens to take its contextual reference from the buildings on the other side of the gallery.[10] This contextual gradation is, however, but one part of what is described by the American writer Ada Louise Huxtable:

> Its aesthetic is loaded with cultural, contextual, symbolic, and historical references. The fact that it does not yield its virtues immediately or universally does not mean that they are not conspicuously present. It is subtle and cerebral; it must be 'read' as both text and artefact. . . . Oddly sectioned, non-supporting columns stand as little morality plays about how technology has undermined the great classical orders. . . . Familiar elements are re-ordered as an expressive aesthetic: what no longer supports now serves the eye.[11]

Gradation is also used by Stirling and Wilford in the contextual design of the Clore Gallery at The Tate, London. Here (Fig. 6.12) the new gallery is artistically graded from the grand Victorian classicism of Smith's portico facing the Thames to the squared panelling of brick and stone of the retained Lodge and the plain brick surfaces of the military hospital blocks to the rear.[12] That is not to say that the new gallery is a mere common denominator of the surrounding buildings, it has its own forceful entrance and a distinctive abstraction of both contextual elements and geometry.

There are several ways by which assimilation can be accommodated into the

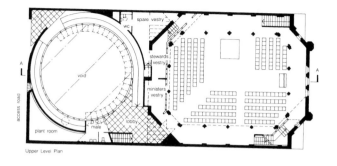

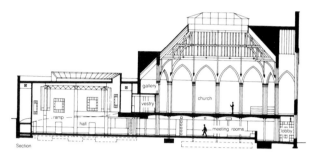

Figure 6.8. United Church, Jewry Street, Winchester. Plincke Leaman and Browning. (a) The church interior is raised to first floor by the insertion of a new floor, and new meeting rooms and facilities take up the ground floor plan. (reproduced from *Building*) (b) New chapel at first floor.

new architecture. We see through mathematics how basic elements can be reflected, transposed, and rotated; through art how it can be overlaid and deformed; and through music where modulation and variation can enrich the primary element. Gabriel Fauré wrote of the phenomenon by which a melody could 'develop and clothe itself in a variety of entertaining harmonies, to change and modulate'.[13]

This is seen in architecture. It is prevalent in the manipulation of classic orders, and other conventional systems, to create mannerist architecture (see section 6.6, 'Modern use of historical details'). It is also used, for example, as a planning device at the Canadian Centre for Architecture in Montreal, Canada. Here, the original Shaughnessy House is reflected across the axis of Boulevard René to appear on a mirrored plan and in a deformed state to form a sculptural reference in Melvin Charney's garden on the history of Montreal (Fig. 6.13). The building complex which forms the Canadian Centre for Architecture is interesting in its own right. The original nineteenth-century house is enclosed on three sides by new accommodation designed by Peter Rose. This successfully breaks the rule that new architecture should normally be smaller than the existing medium. The front facade is detailed as a modern assimilation of the front bays of Shaughnessy House, but these are set away from the house by recessed gaps (see section 5.7, 'A sense of separation') so that the house is framed and made to appear important. The scheme thus becomes an inverted 'egg in the basket' (see section 5.6) with the existing house held as an important and valuable article within the protective frame of the new accommodation.

6.5 Syntax and detail

The details of any building are important; there is no point getting the design idea right if it is going to be developed with details and construction that tell a different story. The new entrance for Conisbrough Castle, for example, was designed to form an association with the idea of a medieval tent (Fig. 6.14), unfortunately the detailing is far too complicated to give this impression, particularly the structure which looks unnecessarily heavy. A building is made up like the syntax of grammar; the written word is read and understood through the correct combination and arrangements of words, phrases, and grammatical constructions. Similarly, a building is appreciated and understood through a coherent combination of detail and structure.

The designer of an extension to a historic building can copy the syntax of the existing building to generate the new architecture; the design assimilates the existing syntax, not necessarily by copying the exact details and materials but by setting up a similar arrangement in a modern medium.

The architectural educationalist Tim Bell[14] uses the analogy of literary criticism to describe the different ways in which the details of a building can hang together to form the total building: 'concurrent construction' is illustrated through the use of synonym, like 'grains of sand on the beach' where all the

Figure 6.9. Chapel of the Apparition, the parish church, Knock, Ireland. The glass enclosure overpowers the existing building.

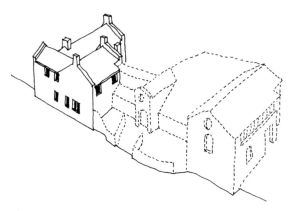

Figure 6.10. Exhibition and Conference Centre for the Brontës, Haworth Parsonage, near Keighley, West Yorkshire. The historic house would be overwhelmed by the size of the proposed extension.

details are similar; '*disarticulated construction*' is illustrated though the use of metaphor, irony, and parody like Robert Venturi's complexity and contradiction in architecture,[15] and Giulio Romano's mannerist, exaggerated, and disjointed use of classic details.[16]

The significance of the detail can also be explored through the idea that a fragment of the building can inform the total. That is, by looking at a particular part (or parts) of an object, we are able to gain an understanding about the whole object. The sight of the hollyhock stylised in stone, for example, reminds us of Frank Lloyd Wright's Barnsdall House. The fragment is a trigger that stimulates a visual recall of the whole. The phenomenon can be used to link the new to the historic site. The introduction of a suitable fragment of history can stimulate the observer into recognising a wider familiarity than is actually stated. The assimilation of the original is hinted at rather than totally fulfilled.

The phenomenon needs to be justified in two ways. First, the fragment has to be selected carefully as only key parts are able to trigger the required response. Second, the response may be general rather than specific: that is, the fragment may induce a response such as 'Roman antiquity' rather than a recall of the specific building from whence the fragment was taken.

It is in the detail that Stirling and Wilford achieve the successful conversion of Albert Dock, Liverpool, into the Tate Gallery. The main entrance (Fig. 6.15) illustrates the masculine strength and robustness of the details for the new elements. These are modern yet retain a sympathetic relationship with the industrial roots of the existing building.

The relationship between the Allen Memorial Gallery and Venturi, Scott Brown and Associates' extension is complex; its primary design source is the intersection of the two plans and the tension which these set up. However, externally the two parts are visually joined by the detailing and colour of materials for the new work, which take their reference from the existing pale marble.

The Ecology Gallery at the Natural History Museum, London, is designed in response to the aim of the exhibition to assist our understanding of the natural world. Ian Ritchie's detailing makes reference between glass walls and water, warm colours and fire, soft flooring and earth, and structural shapes and biology. Accepting that Waterhouse used elements from natural history in some of the terracotta reliefs, nevertheless, the new intervention sets up a dialogue more with the programme for the new display than with the important building in which it weaves around (Fig. 6.16).

6.6 Modern use of historical details

Why is there such adverse criticism of the use of historical details within modern architecture? Why should modern architecture not manipulate historical details and motifs in the same way as has been done so often in the past? There is, after all, no body of criticism against Giulio Romano for his manipulation of classical

Figure 6.11. Sainsbury Wing, The National Gallery, Trafalgar Square, London. Venturi, Scott Brown and Associates. The classical language of William Wilkins's Gallery, 1834–8, is assimilated and graded across the facade of the new wing. (photograph Matt Wargo)

109

details, his outrageous mannerist detailing at the Cortile della Cavallerizza in the Palazzo Ducale, Mantua: we admire Sir Christopher Wren's particularly English interpretation of Renaissance classicism; and we are full of praise for Sir John Soane's extremely personal use of squat and oddly detached historical elements.

Why, then, should not modern architects also make use of historical details; and what are the criteria by which we decide that modern historical details are good or bad? This question falls in part into the trap of a general reaction against change, and also into the tendency to dislike the fashion of our parents; nevertheless, there are other factors. A starting point for this conundrum is the maxim, 'you need to be a good gymnast and an acrobat before you can be a court jester'. That is, you need to be able to perform the standard feat before you can successfully undertake the variations; you need to be able to produce the conventional before you produce the mannerist. In architectural terms this assumes that there is a consensus of opinion as to what is normal, what is standard, what is the basic starting point. We can reasonably say that this, in terms of our classical pedigree, is the common ground of original Greek and Roman architecture; that which still stands in Greece and the Roman Empire, together with that recorded by Vitruvius, Alberti, Palladio, Perrault, and Chambers,[17] and that re-established by modern archaeologists. How can this conventional root in architecture be used in modern design? First, quoting from Tzonis and Lefaivre (1986: 3), *Classical Architecture, The Poetics of Order*, we are 'interested in understanding classical architecture as a coherent system rather than a haphazard collection of shapes and details'.

It is important to recognise that classical architecture has inherent integrity, that it is made up of standard components assembled within accepted codes.[18] Tzonis and Lefaivre devote the core of their book to the origins and basis of this inherent coherence. There are three layers: taxis, genera, and symmetry. Taxis controls the laying out of the plan parts of the building, it provides the characteristic division of spaces. Genera sets out the shape and proportion of that which we now call 'the orders': pedestal, base, shaft, capital, architrave, frieze, cornice. Symmetry refers to the third level of control for the pattern and rhythm of the orders. We thus have a similarity with the landowner who uses a different approach to lay out the trees on his land; he could use a different grid (taxis) to lay out a different species (order) using different proportions and rhythm between the trees (symmetry).

What we see around us are many modern buildings which have used historical features in a haphazard collection of shapes and details. The designers are obviously unaware of the essential coherence within classical architecture. We know, however, that there are examples where classical architecture has been transformed, altered, and modulated to produce what is considered to be successful architecture; in the past by Romano, Wren, Soane, and now Ricardo Bofill (Fig. 6.17), followed by Michael Graves, Charles Jencks, and John Outram.[19] The difference with this type of free-style classicism is that it is carried out with both an understanding of the basic rules and an understanding of the method of transformation by which the primary elements of architecture are modulated into a modern design. The architecture exudes confidence and a *joie de vivre*. Tzonis and Lefaivre recognise that this type of architecture, 'like a witticism, or a joke, is a contained violation of a norm'.

An example where the transformation of historical detailing into modern design is well contained and controlled is the office block, Richmond House, in Whitehall, London. William Whitfield has used a modulated type of Elizabethan architecture together with traditional materials to set the new office building sympathetically into its context (Fig. 6.18).

The important factors are, first, that the transformation is intelligent, be it witty, ironic, or parody, and second, that the violation is contained, that it does not break out of the rules of transformation set by the designer. It is simply not good enough to use historical details as superficial clip-on 'appliqué' to achieve a 'respectable' building. This is no more than a cynical use of history, usually towards some type of planning gain or financial advantage.[20]

Figure 6.12. The Clore Gallery, The Tate, London. Stirling and Wilford. The new wing is graded from the stone classicism of Sidney Smith's Tate Gallery of 1897, to the plain brick panelling of the military hospital to the rear. (photograph Richard Bryant/Arcaid)

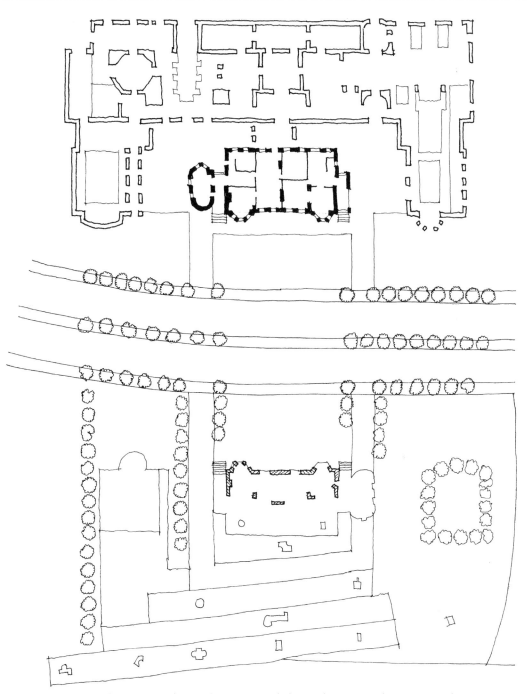

Figure 6.13. Canadian Centre for Architecture and the Sculpture Garden, Montreal. CCA accommodation by Peter Rose; Sculpture Garden by Melvin Charney. The new accommodation wraps around the original house, William Thomas, 1874, to frame it as an important object. The Sculpture Garden is a reflected and deformed version of the plan of the CCA accommodation. (plan drawing James Strike)

113

Figure 6.14. Visitors' Centre, Conisbrough Castle, Yorkshire. The structure is too complicated and heavy to portray the idea of a medieval tent.

Figure 6.15. The Tate Gallery, Albert Dock, Liverpool. James Stirling and Michael Wilford Associates. The detailing and lettering reflect the industrial nature of the original building. (photograph Richard Bryant/Arcaid, courtesy of Stirling and Wilford)

Figure 6.16. Ecology Gallery, Natural History Museum, London. Ian Ritchie. The new design i
generated by the contents of the new exhibition rather than from the Waterhouse building
(photograph Natural History Museum)

Figure 6.17. Housing, Antigoni, Montpellier, France. Ricardo Bofill uses his own ordering of classical elements. (photograph James Strike)

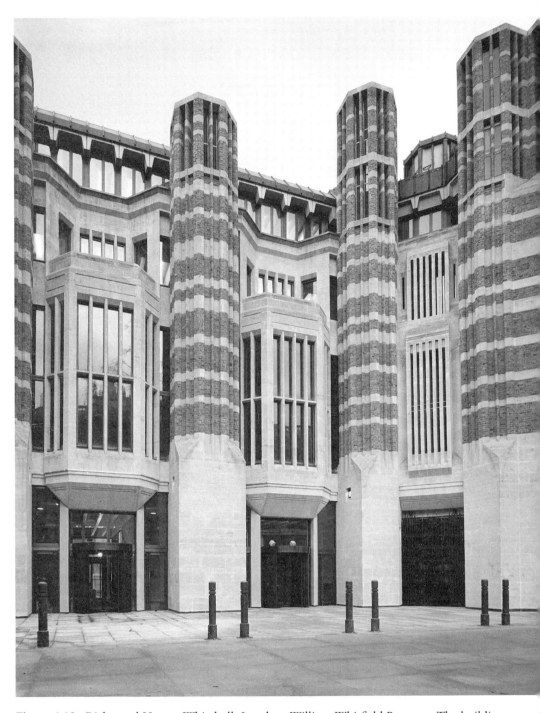

Figure 6.18. Richmond House, Whitehall, London. William Whitfield Partners. The building uses a modern transformation of historical ideas for its response to context. (photograph Jeremy Cockayne/Arcaid, courtesy of William Whitfield Partners.)

118

7

Presence or anonymity

This chapter uses the idea of 'presence or anonymity' to explore the formation of architecture at historic sites. It asks the questions: should the new architecture have a presence at the site or should it be anonymous; should it stand out as an obvious insertion or blend quietly into its surroundings; should it be exuberant or self-effacing? What are the design criteria involved in these questions?

7.1 Blend or blatant

Is the new architecture seen as a statement of our time, or is it built as if constructed some time in the past? Does it recognise that what we collectively refer to as 'history' is made up of layers of time, periods, and styles; that each layer has left its mark on the site for future generations to see (see section 4.4, 'Layers of history')? The street scene of many of our historic cities shows this. The main thoroughfare though the heart of Winchester, for example, retains the line of the original Roman street but now includes Elizabethan, Georgian, Regency, Victorian, Edwardian, and 1960s properties juxtapositioned as a tapestry of evolution. It would seem natural for this process of layering to continue, for our society to add a new layer as a statement of our time, a marker for future generations.

There is, however, a current view about new architecture which seeks to conceal the date of this modern layer; a feeling that it is polite to pretend that what is built today belongs immediately to the past.

Adding a new building into a street scene of mixed periods is, from a historical point of view, relatively straightforward; it adds one more 'coloured sweet' into the mixed bag of 'all-sorts'. Albeit, the architectural difficulties of scale and size still have to be carefully handled.

The new office building for the Harrison Sutton architectural practice in the heart of the historical town of Totnes, Devon, shows how such buildings can have a presence of their own whilst maintaining an appropriate scale and sensitivity in the street scene. The partnership constructed a modern building to link together the Elizabethan House and the Victorian Windeatts Hall. This presents to the street scene along Fore Street a suitably scaled, modern, exposed timber-frame structure clearly separated from the historic buildings on either side by a dark translucent glass wall (Fig. 7.1).

Adding a new piece of architecture to a historical site that is made up of one single style of architecture presents different criteria. Here the modern insertion adds a single 'green' sweet into the bag full of 'raspberry drops'. The equation is different, the weighting different. The modern insertion would be more blatant. The designer and client have to decide if a breakdown of the existing homogeneous nature of the buildings in the area is justified. It is doubtful that the programme for the new brief could justify the change; could it, however, be avoided, could it be concealed within the existing fabric, or displaced to a nearby location? There are some locations where the congruity of the total street or area is so important that it would be wrong to break it. Such places as the splendid Georgian house frontages of the Circus and Royal Crescent in Bath,[1] parts of Regency Leamington Spa,[2] or the formal areas of the 'New Town' of Edinburgh.[3] These areas were built all at one time, they have no palimpsest of history (see section 4.4, 'Layers of history'). The solution is to leave these areas alone, or, if the need should arise, to replace any lost part with an accurate historical replica (see section 7.4, 'Replacing lost fabric').

An unsatisfactory approach to these homogeneous, single-style sites is to attempt a design that is similar but not identical to the existing; to attempt something which is familiar, a sort of historical common denominator. This approach is demonstrated at the Augustinian Priory at Kirkham, Yorkshire. Here a new piece of architecture was added in the 1970s into the remains of a homogeneous twelfth- and thirteenth-century group of Gothic buildings. The new Custodian's Office and Stone Store were designed to blend into the existing monastic group by using the same stone and a traditional form (Fig. 7.2). Nevertheless, the result is sterile: it is neither an accurate historical replica nor a satisfactory piece of twentieth-century architecture. The window and door reveals, for example, are as thin as the outer skin of a modern domestic cavity wall rather than showing the thickness and solidity of a medieval wall. Its location is also unconvincing in its lack of historical precedence – it stands at a cant, neither as a gate-house nor as a convincingly placed lodge (see section 4.1, 'Historical tracks and paths').

It is because such buildings are unconvincing that they draw attention to themselves: there is a sense of disbelief which jolts our mind and triggers an unfortunate second look.

Does the designer wish to remain anonymous or to stamp a name on to the project? Consider, first, the anonymous approach. There is often a fear of change, a fear of something new. The English have a particular trait of reticence. They wish to avoid change, to avoid anything extreme or overt and wish to avoid the shock of the new (a characteristic like the placid English climate which, for all its uncertainties, has no sharp shadows, no grotesque storms or

Figure 7.1. Priory Gate House, 65 Fore Street, Totnes, Devon. Harrison Sutton Partnership have used modern detailing and a small scale for the infill scheme within the context of the historic street. (photograph Harrison Sutton Partnership)

searing sunshine) (see section 2.2, 'Present attitudes'). There is a tendency to prefer the safe and anonymous.

We tend to assume that modern design will produce an overt architectural statement at a historical site. Hopefully, however, the design concepts explained in this book will encourage a more appropriate approach. Paradoxically, there is an aspect of modern lightweight construction that helps to make a new project appear less outrageous and threatening. Section 3.4 ('Buildings as symbols') identified how we tend to form an association between lightweight tensile construction and temporary structures. The examples cited were the temporary cover for the Place des Arènes, Nîmes, (see Fig. 3.4) and the permanent tent cover at Witney, Oxfordshire (see Fig. 5.14). The Witney tent does not appear to be blatant in its surroundings because we assume, subliminally and incorrectly, that it is temporary: it looks like a temporary structure so we assume that it is going to be taken away; it does not pose a permanent threat. Such structures, therefore, appear to blend more naturally into the background than solid buildings of the same size.

The principal argument against the Commissioners' design for the Great Exhibition of 1851 was that it looked too permanent. The design of June 1850 would have taken up most of the country's brickmaking, it is little wonder that *The Times* reported that:

> We are not to have a 'booth', nor a mere timber shed, but a solid, substantial edifice of brick, iron, and stone, calculated to endure the wear and tear of the next hundred years. In fact, a building is about to be erected in Hyde Park as substantial as Buckingham Palace. Can anyone be weak enough to suppose that a building erected on such a scale will ever be removed?[4]

The title 'Crystal Palace', which was attributed later to Paxton's design, conveys the delicacy of construction; modern but transparent, light, and removable.

It takes more confidence for a designer to see the new architecture as having a strong character of its own. This may have been acceptable in the past (see section 2.1, 'Views of history'), we overlook the audacious nature of the early Renaissance buildings built in London, we see them now as part of the overall mulch of history (see section 3.9, 'The significance of time'). However, present attitudes are different, they are more conservative. The Clore Gallery at the Tate, London, for example (see Fig. 6.12) was considered to be too overt when it opened in 1984; it was seen as a mid-European design rather than something for London.

There must always be room for divergent talent and lateral thinking, room for schemes which go against the common rules. The Italians and the French are more confident in the use of modern architecture, more likely to execute buildings that stir up debate and lead eventually to a change in the 'spirit of the age' (see section 2.2, 'Present attitudes').

Figure 7.2. Custodian's Office, Kirkham Priory, Yorkshire. Department of the Environment, Ancient Monuments Branch. The use of traditional materials and construction does not always achieve sympathetic results. (photograph Caryl Stanley)

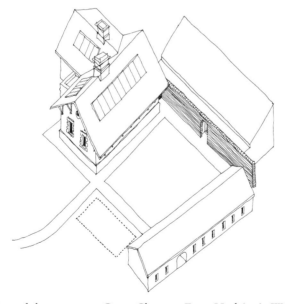

Figure 7.3. Extension of the museum, Great Chesters Fort, Hadrian's Wall. Exploratory proposals for new accommodation concealed behind a landscape wall. Original museum by Norman Shaw. And a new block to regularise the external space between the existing buildings into a formal courtyard. (scheme and drawing James Strike)

123

7.2 Concealed architecture

Some projects deliberately aim to conceal the new architecture. It is this conscious intention to hide the new building which acts as the generator for the design of the scheme.

A simple approach is to conceal the new accommodation behind an existing wall. There are numerous examples. However, as these usually involve such mundane projects as public lavatories or a custodian's office, they get little publicity. The facilities discreetly accessed through the courtyard walls at Carisbrooke Castle, for example, are noteworthy in that they are unnoticeable. The approach can be used to conceal larger buildings; the only criteria being that the wall has to be sufficiently high to cover the new architecture, and that nothing is done to the existing wall, particularly to its copings, to indicate that it is no longer standing as a simple garden wall.

The idea can be extended through designing a new wall rather than using existing fabric to conceal the new architecture, that is, the facing facade of the new building is detailed in such a way as to represent an existing garden wall. The proposal to extend the museum at Great Chesters Fort on Hadrian's Wall is an interesting example. The existing museum was built in 1900 by Norman Shaw; a charming little pavilion designed in the 'Tuscan' style. This still houses the various artefacts in their original black wooden display cabinets, and the catalogued stones still stand in rows along the original shelves. The whole thing, building and contents, survives as an untouched example of curatorial practice at the beginning of the century. The museum and its contents are now seen as a historic conservation item in its own right. Two problems arise: how to absorb additional artefacts into the collection, and how to present a meaningful interpretation of the site. Both have to be achieved without destroying the architectural, historical, and curatorial integrity of the existing museum. The proposal is to construct an extension to the museum behind a new 'landscape wall' (Fig. 7.3). This is arranged to keep the Norman Shaw building as a complete entity in its own right, to preserve it as a object that can be seen in the round, as if viewing a piece of sculpture.

Restoration of Woodbridge Lodge similarly uses the device of concealing the new accommodation behind a new 'garden' wall. The design allows the gatehouse to Rendlesham Hall,[5] Suffolk, to be upgraded to suit modern needs. The scheme returns the Gothic folly to its original pure shape by removing the 1940s flat roof extensions and placing this accommodation, together with additional space, behind the new 'garden wall' (Fig. 7.4). Here, the arc of the wall not only conceals the new accommodation but also provides a backdrop to the lodge; it forms a sense of enclosure to enhance the importance and delicacy of the historic folly. The confident scheme by Hugh Pilkington shows the value of an interested and informed client[6] and the advantages of early and close liaison with the various planning bodies concerned.

The proposal for an extension of the Dulwich College Picture Gallery develops the idea from actual concealment to implied concealment. The gallery, built in

1811–14, is of international importance, both for its contents and for John Soane's Gallery in which they are housed. The international competition, sponsored by *Country Life* and administered by the Royal Institute of British Architects, required additional accommodation to provide modern facilities for picture-framing, workshops, education, retail, and a café. It attracted over 350 entries. The winning entry by Zetek and O'Neill was simple yet strong. The main axis of the existing galleries is extended into the gardens to form the new accommodation.[7] These new rooms are enclosed on either side by discontinuous walls which not only conceal the central lightweight steel and glass structure, but also set up a relationship between the new rooms and the landscape through gaps strategically placed along their length. The walls belong, in one sense, to the gardens and as such do not compete with the distinctive style of the existing buildings.

Another approach is to conceal the new accommodation below ground. This is potentially expensive, but may be the only way forward for sites where the setting allows no other solution. The famous view of Queen's House, Greenwich, with its important Renaissance symmetry and formal lawns down to the Thames, should not be altered. The need for expansion of the National Maritime Museum, therefore, led to the proposal by the Building Design Partnership, to sink a two-storey building beneath the lawns with the Neptune Hall extended to include an adjacent courtyard concealed by a glass dome.

The headquarters building for the RMC Group, designed by Edward Cullinan Associates, is concealed under landscape roofs to minimise its impact on the Surrey green belt. The subterranean scheme joins together three existing houses. The large areas of garden landscapes are imaginatively handled by the landscape architects Derek Lovejoy and Partners to define the various external spaces of English landscape and to create the internal sunken Italian Renaissance enclosures (Fig. 7.5).[8]

It is also possible to reduce the impact of new architecture in a historical setting by use of camouflage. In the way that large army tanks, aircraft hangars, and ships were concealed during the war, so modern buildings can similarly be made to blend into their surroundings. It is interesting to observe that camouflage became a recognised art form during the First World War; recognised by Picasso and his colleagues as contributing to, and derived from, avant-garde movements such as cubism.[9] There are no specific examples where large surface colour camouflage has been used as a positive design ingredient of a conservation project; nevertheless, this would be a reasonable approach to take. There are two design principles in the use of camouflage, and both could be useful for new architecture at a historic site. First, to give the same tonality to the new building as the historic background: as, for example, in the simple detail of concealing the shape of a new door into St Peter's Church in Vere Street, Westminster, by painting out the shape of the whole original opening in the same dark tone. Second, to break down the shape and surface of the new building to coincide with the shape and pattern of the background. This idea of giving the new building the same size and grain as the surroundings is discussed in section 4.6

('Grain and matrix'). Surface decoration in colour and texture has been an English interest since the Middle Ages,[10] it can be used either to extenuate or defuse the shape and form of an object. The phenomenon is seen also in the paintings of Matisse, where, in such paintings as *Nature morte, Seville II*, the surface decoration of the tablecloth and chair covers is so strong that the individual shapes of the articles congeal into one.

This leads on to the concept of 'layering' the various historical levels on a site. This issue was discussed previously in section 4.4 ('Layers of history'). The new modern layer can be considered as a screen over the face of the historical fabric, a new partial layer acting like a filter, lattice, or lacework to allow glimpses of the original. The new glass wall at Liverpool Street Station, London, demonstrates this (Fig. 7.6): the filigree detailing forms interesting shafts of light, shadow, and distortion over the Victorian structure. It recalls the image of partial transparency experienced when looking at a building through a line of silver birch trees.

7.3 Preservation or restoration

This section considers design implications related to the repair of historic buildings. The intention is not to examine the particular materials and techniques used in preservation and restoration, as these are already covered in specialist books which explain each of the specific skills: a good starting point being the English Heritage series, *Practical Building Conservation*, vols 1–5 (Ashurst and Ashurst 1988). The subject at hand is to do with policy and design criteria. The questions to be answered are: What approach should be adopted for the repair of the historic fabric? How much repair work should be done? How far should it go?

A clerk of works on one site was so concerned to achieve a neat, solid, and straight finished building that he had to be restrained from issuing instructions to take down the whole of the historic fabric; he wanted to be sure that it was correctly and soundly rebuilt. There is a natural tendency to do too much, it takes restraint when taking down defective fabric not to remove too much, to remember that the fabric is historic and cannot be replaced. John Ruskin, writing in 1849, recognised the value of the actual fabric: 'How many pages of doubtful record might we not often spare, for a few stones left one upon another?'[11]

The primary objective should be to preserve the fabric as it is found, to undertake the preservation without taking the historic fabric to pieces, or, if unavoidable, to take down only the minimum amount of fabric needed to undertake the repair. Although new building work can be considered as a recording of the past, it is no longer the actual historic fabric, the facsimile is not the same as the original and should not be presented as such. It is necessary to retain the 'face' of the historic fabric.[12] The loss of fabric is important , but equally important is a change of appearance. Dinah Casson likens historic fabric

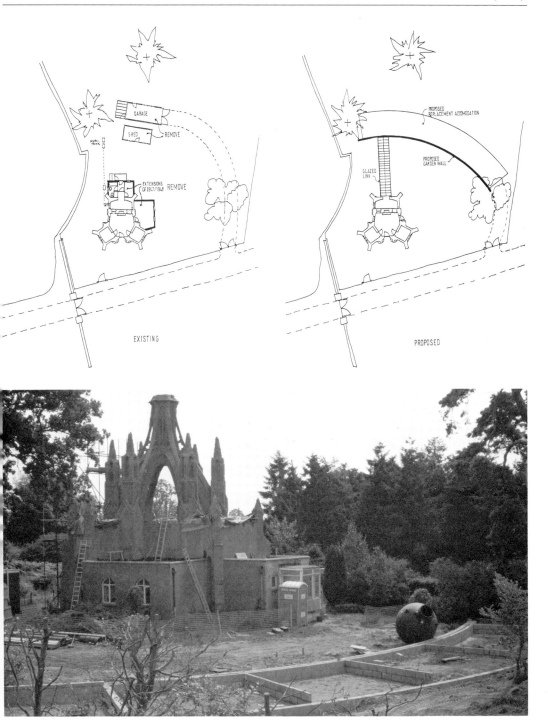

Figure 7.4. Woodbridge Lodge, Rendlesham, Suffolk. Hugh Pilkington. (a) Existing and proposed plans. (drawings Hugh Pilkington) (b) The arc of new accommodation (under construction) enhances the space and importance of the existing folly. (photograph James Strike)

to 'a well worn and mended garment', she sees conservation as a continuous process and compares the repair of old buildings to 'a valuable lace garment or an altar frontal for which you would continue to do all you can to avoid renewal of its parts'.[13] Casson's restoration of 29 Bedford Square into Headquarters for the Society of Designers avoids the usual coy idea of interiors for historic buildings. She avoids wall to wall carpets and brass light switches which neither recognise the actual history of Georgian candles and coal fires nor provide modern design for modern needs.

There will, however, be occasions where it is appropriate to take out an element of the existing fabric and replace it with something new. The west range of the Blackfriars in Gloucester provides a suitable explanation. Some time in the 1960s the medieval archway leading into the refectory was bricked in with a new timber door and window which cut into the stone mouldings (Fig. 7.7). We have to accept, in spite of our desire to retain as much as possible of the monument's history, that there are some items of work executed in the past which are simply crass; things which are not worthy of preservation; acts which are detrimental to, rather than representational of, the time at which they were carried out. Such decisions require a strong understanding of history and architecture.

The debate as to whether to preserve as found or restore with new construction has always to address the question: why does the existing fabric have to be disturbed? A guiding policy is to assume the fabric to be 'innocent until proved guilty',[14] that it can stay where it is unless there is something terminally wrong with it.

If the conservation of the monument has to include renewal of fabric, then the new work should be identifiable. Article 12 of the Venice Charter states:

> Replacements of missing parts must integrate harmoniously with the whole, but at the same time must be distinguishable from the original so that restoration does not falsify the artistic or historical evidence.

Many different methods have been used to identify the new work, some more suitable than others. For example, tiny glass beads were added to the mortar repairs at Byland Abbey; these, however, reflected the headlights of passing cars to give the monument an unfortunate glow.

If each repair is separately identified, then a sequence of repairs builds up to tell the story of the site (see section 4.4, 'Layers of history'). The stones of the church of Santos Stephano, Bologna, show all the traces of its history, the earliest invaders, the Romans, Visigoths, Byzantines, Lombards, and the Franks.

We can, as a precursor to section 7.5 ('Building history'), see how this device may be used to generate the design of new buildings. It is used by Rock Townsend for the Angel Square Office Block in Islington, where the brick elevations are loaded with contextural references such as broken arches and other impressions of the layers of an invented history.[15] It is also used in Branson Coates's design of the Wall Leisure Club, Tokyo (Fig. 7.8). The main facade consists of a new 'quattrocento' wall which artificially recreates layers of history.

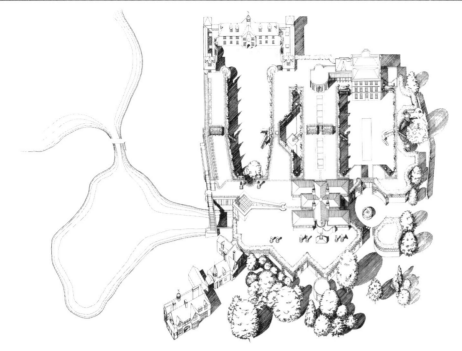

Figure 7.5. Offices for RMC Headquarters, Surrey. Edward Cullinan. (a) Line drawing of the new accommodation formed beneath the roof garden landscapes. (plan courtesy of Edward Cullinan) (b) View across the lawns. (photograph Martin Charles)

129

7.4 Replacing lost fabric

This section looks at the use of new architecture to replace parts of a historic monument which are now missing – parts which, for one reason or another, have been lost. There is, of course, the common rule that missing parts should not be replaced, that the monument should be conserved 'as found'; that to reconstruct lost pieces would confuse our comprehension of the monument as a document of the events that have formed its history.

Nevertheless, there are specific cases where replacement of lost fabric should be considered. One such case is to re-establish the visual coherence of the architecture. Consider, for example, the hypothetical need to replace one bay of the thirty houses that make up the Royal Crescent at Bath (see section 7.1, 'Blend or blatant'). The Crescent as a whole reads as a complete unit. It is this completeness which forms its beauty; it is the repetition of the 114 identical Ionic columns which creates the complete whole, gives a sense of coherence and architectural integrity to the great curve. It would, therefore, be appropriate to replicate any part that was destroyed in order to preserve this coherence. The first-floor windows of the Crescent were lowered in the early nineteenth century to improve the interiors; only No. 1 has been restored to the original appearance intended by John Wood the Younger. Roger White of The Georgian Society takes the view that any repairs carried out should restore the windows to the original design;[16] this, however, would not improve visual coherence and would remove part of the evidence of the history of the Crescent.

These decisions are based more on aesthetic considerations than on historical or archaeological factors. Justification cannot normally be made to rebuild a missing part of a monument on the grounds of historical data or archaeological evidence. Accepting that the decision is usually aesthetic, then a useful aid for the decision-making process is to ask the basic question: what does the existing fabric look like? If the answer is that it looks unfinished, that it looks as if it is waiting to be completed, then the response should be to rebuild the missing part. If, however, the existing fabric can be seen as a picturesque ruin, incomplete but an attractive object in its own right, then leave it as it is.

A useful starting point from which to test this hypothesis is Gill Chitty's paper 'A prospect of ruins'.[17] This paper (previously described in section 2.3) traces the stages through which a building passes to become a ruin. We can use this classification to look at several monuments. Chiswick House, for example, is at 'stage 1' of the scale, that is, a building which has not yet begun to fall to pieces; here is a building where we would have no qualms about replacing a rotten window, rebuilding a crumbling parapet, or even renewing the roof coverings. At the other end of Gill Chitty's scale is a building such as Corfe Castle, Dorset, a building which has passed through all of the stages to become a ruin; here we would not contemplate straightening up or rebuilding the walls, or replacing the windows. Thus we have a system which says that the more decayed the monument, the less appropriate it is to rebuild it, and vice versa: the newer the building looks, the more appropriate it is to rebuild it.

Figure 7.6. Liverpool Street Station, London. Architecture and Design Group, British Rail. A filter of modern glazing in front of the existing structure. (photograph James Strike)

What happens in the central grey area of the time scale? Consider, for example, the Garrison Church at Portsmouth (Fig. 7.9). This is primarily a fine fourteenth-century structure on the site of the Domus Dei hospital founded in 1212. The church was taken over for military use and in 1866 underwent major restoration and alterations by G. E. Street. The roof and fittings of the nave were destroyed by an incendiary bomb in 1941. The question, which has lingered around for many years, is: should the interior of the nave be reroofed to protect the friable stone mouldings and important military memorials? The nave has not not reached 'stage 5' of Chitty's classification, that is, it has not yet become a visual or picturesque ruin. Reaction to the external appearance is that it is 'waiting to be completed, the gable end is complete and the builders have, for some reason or another, gone away'. We get the same sense of expectation when we see a bridge under construction and the two sections are coming together in mid-span. It would, therefore, seem reasonable to reroof the nave.

The question then moves forward: should it be a modern roof or should the Victorian roof be rebuilt? The nave has lost its High Victorian timber fittings and windows and so replacing Street's roof has to be seen either as providing an incomplete redundant church interior, or as the first step towards a total recasting of the Victorian interior. The present interior is open to the sky and is used as a quiet place of shelter; an alternative approach would, therefore, be to complete the building with a new tinted glass roof detailed externally to create an association with the rolls of a traditional lead roof (see section 5.5, 'New roofs and umbrellas'). A modern glass roof would not only retain the nave as a ruin and a memorial to the events of the Second World War, but also create a useful covered space with the feeling of an outside arcade.

Lulworth Castle in Dorset is a similar case. The castle is not in fact a defensive stronghold but an elaborate pretence built in 1611 as a hunting lodge for Lord Howard, a courtier of James I who was passionate for the deer-hunt. The house was burnt down in 1929. The decision to reconstruct the roof was taken, not only to protect the interior where modern techniques of restoration will be left uncovered and exhibited,[18] but also to recreate the elaborate skyline of the 'castle' roofs so that the monument can again make its intended contribution to the landscape.

Such decisions are visual and architectural rather than chronological or archaeological. It is interesting to observe that the conservation movement is highly respected for its knowledge of history and archaeology but is less confident about architectural quality.

Another reason for restoring lost fabric is to gain a better understanding of the monument. There are occasions when the historic fabric, which has come down to us as a particular monument, is so incomplete or disjointed that it is meaningless; it is impossible to understand the remaining masonry without diligent research and considerable knowledge of the period. It may be argued that reconstruction of some of the missing parts should be carried out for their educational value. This approach has been scorned over the last fifty years as lacking authenticity, although prior to this it was carried out on quite a big scale.

Figure 7.7. Refectory Range, Blackfriars, Gloucester. Should everything of the past be preserved?

What we now see as the complete Great Hall at Dartington Hall, Devon, was rebuilt up from the ruined walls. Interestingly, there were no record drawings when this was carried out in the early 1930s, but subsequent discovery of some early drawings has shown that the interpretation based on ghost-like chases and a degree of practical experience has proved to be correct.[19]

These are difficult decisions. Graham Fairclough[20] of English Heritage has addressed the problem through a pragmatic listing of the pros and cons, such as education, new use, and financial income, versus historical authenticity and building costs. However, even with this methodology, the data for each specific site have to be assessed. The architectural criteria can be isolated for exploration. First, historical monuments often consist of empty shells, the timber floors being more prone to fire and decay: to replace these missing horizontal elements has the advantage of dividing up these misleadingly tall volumes to give a clearer idea of the original spaces. Second, reconstruction can allow the visitor to get close up to the interesting parts of an interior such as carved fireplaces. Third, reroofing a monument will help to protect the interior. And fourth, the architectural criteria, which have previously been covered, help to decide on the completion of a coherent architectural statement or the retention of a picturesque ruin.

The educational benefit of rebuilding history has, in exceptional cases, led to the complete reconstruction of a lost building. This was done at Mount Grace Priory, Yorkshire, where one of the monks' houses was rebuilt, including period furniture, to examine and explain the Carthusian way of life.[21] The new cell block stands out in the ruins of the cloister range as a new but accurate replica. This clarity of what is rebuilt and what is original is less clear in the living history museum buildings of Williamsburg in America.

To rebuild history purely to create a new commercial use lacks a commitment to our time and negates the potential of good modern architecture to achieve the same results.

7.5 Building history

This section looks at the idea of building new architecture as a replica of history; that is, new buildings designed and built to look as if they have always been there.

What are the problems of building new history? There have been times in the past when it was fashionable to use historical styles to generate the design of new buildings. Renaissance architecture was, as the name implies, a 'rebirth' of Greek and Roman buildings. Similarly, the Victorian 'revivals' of Greek, Gothic, Egyptian, among others, were also a renewal of interest in past styles. An important characteristic has to be noted. Although these revivals made use of previous architectural styles, they did not produce replicas of the earlier buildings; their interest in the past was not to recast the earlier buildings but to use them as a stimulus for new designs. Thus Renaissance buildings used the

Figure 7.8. The Wall Leisure Club, Nishi-Azabu, Tokyo. Branson Coates. A frontage detailed to portray a pretence of history. (photograph Valentine Hawes)

135

classical elements of base, column, capital, frieze, pediment, etc., not in a truly Greek or Roman way but for innovation in a seventeenth-century manner.

It is natural that the Renaissance buildings should look different to their predecessors; they were, after all, a result of different needs, and improved building techniques such as the evolution of large span timber roofs, and were, incidentally, often based only on conjectural drawings of the Greek and Roman originals. Similarly, Victorian buildings were stimulated by philosophical and religious interest in the past, rather than a wish to create exact copies of the earlier buildings. There is considerable difference between a medieval Gothic church and a Gothic revival church of the Victorian period: the assembly of parts changes from the regulated medieval structure of French cathedrals to the interlapping and irregular build-up of the churches of such architects as Butterfield and Webb; tracery moves towards flat plate surfaces, and structural iron makes possible the open and tenuous interiors of churches such as St George's, Everton.[22] Again, it takes little skill to recognise the difference between an Ionic temple of the third to fifth century BC and the Ionic Greek revival churches of Alexander Thomson.[23]

These revivalist buildings were like new births that showed a resemblance of their forefathers: there was a sense of evolution in their design. These are not replicas, they are not like the genetically engineered 'Replicant' people manufactured to form the servile community in Ridley Scott's film *Bladerunner*.

There is today a difference in the new architecture which is categorised as 'revival'. We now see not only architecture that uses the past to create a modern historical style, now referred to as 'post-modern' or 'free-style classicism' (see section 6.6, 'Modern use of historical details'), but also new buildings that have been built as complete replicas of historical architecture. These replicas have been tagged 'pastiche'.

Why is the term 'pastiche' considered to be detrimental? The roots of its meaning are 'a work of art that mixes styles and materials', this implies a lively composition, as in the musical term *capriccio*. It has also an alternative meaning, 'a work of art in the style of another artist'. Today, the term 'pastiche' has taken on a harder use of this meaning to imply 'a new work which replicates an earlier piece of art'. We see today buildings that are not simply 'in the style of' but in fact 'copies' of previous architectural designs. This is a new phenomenon, it is not a traditional approach as exponents of this school of design would have us believe.

This approach is now used in the misunderstanding that it is going to produce something safe, a building that is non-threatening because it is familiar: 'We like old buildings, we have grown accustomed to them, they are old friends.' The problem is that these historical look-alikes are new, they are not old friends. These buildings are made of instantaneous history, they have no sense of evolution, they have no story line, they add nothing to the architectural debate. It is this limited content which restricts our enjoyment and appraisal, the observer has no choice of critical approach.[24]

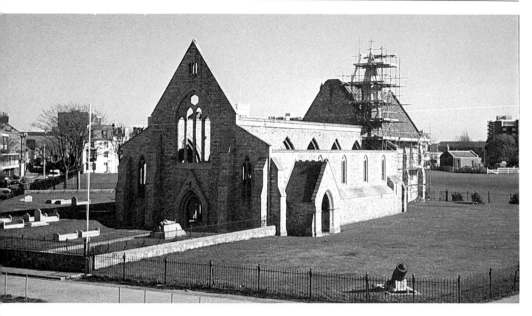

Figure 7.9. Garrison Church, Portsmouth. The part ruin looks as if it is waiting to be completed. (photograph James Strike)

Figure 7.10. Arcaid photographic studio, The Factory, Kingston, London. Pierre D'Avoine. The new facilities are set in opposition to the grid of the existing structure. (photograph Richard Bryant/Arcaid)

137

Another problem is that old buildings usually look worn and slightly muddled whilst these new buildings are of one period and look clean and orderly. Attempts have been made to create artificial surface patina and to build in a sense of historical evolution. This is seen in pub interiors and in new buildings, such as the Islington Office Block and The Wall Leisure Club (see discussion on p. 128).

The word 'authentic' comes into the discussion. One of the villagers in Marcel Pagnol's novel *Jean de Florette* overhears the doctor describing his furniture as 'authentic'. A villager asks, 'What is this thing "authentic"?'; he does not understand that it is not an object, to him everything is real, the objects about him are straightforward, there is no need to describe them as genuine. However, time and culture have gradually fostered copies and deception, and a nuance has crept into the word. 'Authentic' used to mean that the object was made contemporaneously with its style, that it is not a copy, now 'this is an authentic copy' means that it is an accurate copy, the historical details of the replica are correct.

We may observe that the vast range of constructional techniques that are now available makes it easier to produce dishonest buildings. Traditional construction leads naturally to honest architecture, but modern construction allows the architect to get up to all sorts of tricks and visual deceits. Buildings prior to the Industrial Revolution were predominantly of load-bearing masonry construction. The higher the wall, the thicker the wall, and this thickness showed at the window and door reveals. The growth of the structural frame has led to non-loadbearing wall construction and this has made possible thin brick or stone cladding, sometimes as thin as 50mm. The window and door reveals get reduced, the whole frontage becomes flattened, historical detail and accuracy are lost, and sunlight shadows reduced. The result is no more than a thin veneer of historical detailing made up of clip-on construction. History can now be used as a wallpaper covering over modern construction and a modern interior.

The idea of truth is also part of the discussion. Immanuel Kant sets two classes of truth: first, *a priori*, independent of experience and valid by reason of definition (a quadruped is a four-legged animal); and second, *a posteriori*, dependent on previous experience, true or false according to how it is observed (it would be sensible to cross the road further up).[25] Conservation is concerned with the latter type of truth, that is, with decisions based on previous experience. It is these previous experiences which inform and formulate our predilections and ideas.

We see then that criticism of the details of these revival buildings is bounded by the architectural approach of the architect concerned. We cannot say that Ricardo Bofill's details of the houses at Antigoni (see Fig. 6.17) are incorrect because they do not conform to Palladio; this was not his idea. We cannot say that Terry Farrell's Charing Cross scheme fails because it not a clear expression of its structure spanning over the railway platforms; again, Farrell's theories were different, he was more concerned that the building assimilated the idea of engine shed and terminus. However, we can reprimand a revival building if its commitment to an architectural idea is unclear or if the details are inconsistent within the criteria which it sets up.

7.6 Opposites

The final section of this chapter looks at the concept of 'opposites' and its role in giving presence rather than anonymity to the new architecture. Doing something opposite would at first seem contrary to the notion of trying to set up some sort of empathy between the new architecture and the historic site. Here, however, we have to distinguish between 'opposite' and 'difference'. We all know of examples where a new building is totally different to its historic setting: a 1960s sectional-timber gymnasium built up against a fine Victorian school, or the squared up concrete frame and panel office block built alongside Bangor University. These are disassociated, random, and unrelated. With 'opposites', however, we need to focus on 'the far ends of a rainbow', or the 'extreme ends of the same idea': these ends are attached by the same centre, and in architectural terms, each end belongs to the same common idea. It is salutary to use an actual example. The architectural photographers Arcaid have formed a modern studio within an industrial building (Fig. 7.10). Pierre D'Avoine's modern insertion to form the dark-room and storage is based deliberately on a geometry that is in opposition to the existing building. The congruence of the new and existing structures lies in their directional use of the structural grid. Each uses the grid in a different way but this common interest holds them together.

Similarly, Derek Latham's scheme for the conversion of Old Mill at Oundle into a hotel complex uses the same concept of 'opposites' (see Fig. 4.6). The curved geometry of the new block is set in deliberate antithesis against the orthogonal geometry of the existing mill; geometry is the common denominator.

Several architectural attributes can be used as the common denominator in this design concept: new lightweight architecture in opposition to existing heavy-weight masonry, or new transparency in antithesis to impenetrable existing fabric. An unusual example is seen in the new International Conference Centre discreetly built alongside, and partially beneath, Dublin Castle. Part of this new facility interlocks with some fine and delicate Georgian interiors, and so the decision was made to express the new fittings and furniture as 'thick' timber construction in opposition to the thin and delicate Georgian detailing. This gives it a separate identity, although the decision to give the new timber detailing a half-rounded profile, to form an association with the medieval masonry and round towers of the earlier parts of the castle, has given the new fittings and furniture an appearance reminiscent of the early 1940s.[26]

What is interesting in these schemes that use the design concept of 'opposites' is not the visual statement of the opposing ends but the architectural characteristic that forms the common denominator.

8

The way forward

8.1 Duty of care

Historic buildings are a valuable and irreplaceable commodity; their owners, private, institutional, or government, have a duty of care to look after them. Unlike other valuable commodities, they cannot be replaced if lost or damaged.

The Venice Charter (Article 4) states: 'It is essential to the conservation of monuments that they be maintained on a permanent basis'. And Michael Heseltine, at the launch of English Heritage Annual Report in 1991, emphasised: 'a new prominence to the concept of "sustainability", however much we want to enjoy our heritage, we have an overriding duty to preserve it and hand it on to others'. He recognised that heritage is becoming more important in people's lives:

> a growing recognition that conservation is an important part of the quality of life. People respond to a historic environment, not because it offers a nostalgic retreat into the past, but because it contributes to the quality of life now.

Historic buildings and monuments, together with their settings and landscapes, belong to the country as well as their owners.

There is a danger when undertaking building work at a historic site that we consider the project in the same way as any other building work. However, it is important to recognise, right from the outset, that building at historic sites requires a different approach. Architecture for conservation needs a specific attitude. Projects should not be set up and assessed against the usual set of pragmatic values, they specifically require additional time, additional finance, and particular skills.

8.2 Market forces

We have seen in section 1.2 ('Identifying the problem') that the increase in the interest of history has put our monuments and our historic areas under threat; leisure time is now a larger part of people's lives, visitor numbers are on the increase, and people are prepared to travel further and to pay more in order to work in interesting historic towns. All of this engenders a pressure for change.

At the same time, economic change, linked closely with development of technology, and changes in social behaviour, have caused many historic buildings to become unsuitable for twentieth-century needs. There are many nineteenth-century industrial mills now looking for an economic future; many large Victorian churches find it impractical to stay open; and many country estates are having to reconsider the financing of the family properties. All of this, again, engenders a pressure for change.[1]

Creating new architecture for conservation projects presents a particular problem; it is easy to go through the conventional pragmatic steps, but more is required. The design criteria needed for a conservation project cut across many more disciplines. Randolph Langenbach of the University of California writes:[2]

> With the construction of a new building the social, cultural, and even, sometimes, the symbolic meaning exists on completion of the project; this is achieved through the act of the design. With a historic building there is no clean blank slate. Buildings which society has deemed to be historic have meaning, and the designer's understanding of this meaning has everything to do with the success of the results of the interventions.[3]

The designer has to evaluate and explore this meaning in the design process.

Langenbach illustrates this through criticism of the conversion, in the 1970s, of the Washington DC Railway Terminal into a Visitors' Centre for the city. This 'severed the station from its still active use as a terminus by moving the trains to a miserable shed at the rear', and 'the main concourse was cut up and filled with weak and underscaled exhibits which ruined the majesty of the space'.[4] We have to ensure that market forces are not taken on their immediate face value but are considered on a wider and long-term perspective.

A scheme that is calculated solely on financial gain, and does not encompass the conservation and cultural aspects, may well fail in the long term. People are more selective than we give them credit for and will prefer to visit projects that have a sense of place. Successful schemes are those that respect the original use of the site. The new architecture helps to reveal the building's history, its identity is retained.

It therefore follows that the existing characteristics of the historic building – that is, those elements of scale, arrangement of spaces, etc., that are inherent in the original use – can limit the options of change. The change of use of London's County Hall[5] into a hotel, for example, raises doubts about the balance between short-term finance against architectural and long-term considerations. Its imposing elevation on to the Thames, and its formal council chambers and circular corridors of power, all speak of authority and civic pride. It is a shame to wash this into the soft comfort and opulence of an expensive hotel.[6]

The architectural intervention at the Albert Dock, Liverpool, does respect the original use of the building. Stirling and Wilford's conversion of this nineteenth-century warehouse into the Tate Gallery of Liverpool adopts a strong and heavy iconography for its detailing (see Fig. 6.15). These new images are obviously modern but retain the similar robust and purposeful feeling of the brick and cast-iron warehouse (see section 6.5, 'Syntax and detail').

New architecture that forms additional accommodation at or by a historic building can be used to create finance for the restoration of the building. There is, however, a danger that the pressure of market forces will be used as the single criterion to calculate and justify the amount of 'enabling development' needed to fund the restoration. This is seductive and dangerous. It is essential that the optimum size of the new development is arrived at from the design process which is generated from the historic building and its contents. If the financial equation can be balanced within this restraint, then all is well: if not, then a different approach has to be found.

Restoration of Hankelow Hall, an early eighteenth-century country house in Cheshire, can thus be funded by 'enabling development' proposed for an open site at the rear of the house (Fig. 8.1). The optimum size of this scheme was ascertained from the design of modern housing formed on the idea of a stable-block. There is evidence of outbuildings in this area, although no specific details can be established. The scheme is a modern interpretation of the form and 'footprint' of what might have been there.

Finally, market forces relate to conservation through the world of insurance. The decision to restore the National Trust property Uppark, Sussex, after the fire in 1989, was influenced by the insurance cover. The policy allowed finance to rebuild that which was lost, but not for any other form of construction to pursue an alternative presentation of the remains (see section 5.5, 'New roofs and umbrellas'). The Conservation Practice, who were responsible for rebuilding the house, used the most thorough and up-to-date techniques for the salvage, investigation, recording, and assembly of the works. The cost of these modern methods was expensive and insurance companies are now looking to align premiums more closely to the new costs of this type of conservation. We will be faced with different rates for conservation rebuild as apart from conventional types of reconstruction.

The whole world of risk and insurance is taking on a higher profile in conservation. We have to ensure that the requirements of fire protection, theft, and personal safety do not lead to physical changes which destroy that which is to be protected. We have to explore alternative methods of management, security patrol, and new types of agreement with the Fire Brigade, so as to modify the physical intervention. English Heritage is, for example, undertaking such trials at Osborne House on the Isle of Wight, where controlled management of visitors is used in preference to fire compartmentation of the building.

8.3 Commissioning the project

The first requirement is to clarify the need, to test the aims against the numerous immediate and long-term pressures. This requires the right group of people to appraise the project: archaeologists, historians, curators, architects, finance managers, marketing agents, presentation artists, and administrators need to be represented. At this early stage the team also needs people who, in management classification, are known as 'plants', those capable of lateral thought and injecting fresh ideas; such people have the ability to widen the options and see alternative ways forward.

It is recognised that this group will represent many vested and conflicting interests: the marketing manager may want a more direct type of presentation; the historian nothing changed; the landscape designer rough grass and picturesque ivy; and the archaeologist clean and repointed walls. However, their views at this stage should be advisory, their cases need to be heard, but the final decision has to be taken at a higher level, and by a smaller group. Leadership needs to be well informed but purposeful and broad shouldered. It is no use relying on a compromise, this is no way to achieve good architecture.

The objectives, thus identified, are then encapsulated as 'the brief' which is to be given to the various members of the design team. This is usually written in a 'prescriptive' tone: Library 200 square metres, Education room 40 square metres, etc. It would, however, be more helpful to produce this brief in a more 'descriptive form'. This should open with a philosophical statement about the overall intention for the site; it could use such phrases as 'the landscaping and new architecture should strengthen the masculine and authoritative characteristics of the Norman tower', or 'the site will be returned to the eighteenth-century "picturesque" '. The designer then knows the overall aim for the new architecture. Similarly, the brief for the component parts of the development should also be descriptive: they should explain the function and performance of each area rather than giving a bland statement of the supposed square metres. The designer is then able to deduce far more from these descriptive words, to understand the performance and characteristics required, and to match these into the specially commissioned buildings. Research is not just a matter of collecting data, it requires interpretation, it requires a philosophical assessment which gives the data a context. Mary Midgley, in *Wisdom, Information and Wonder*, writes:

> Without a context, and in particular a moral context, for the
> interpretation of knowledge, our relentless accumulation of information
> is pointless and wisdom impossible.[7]

Designing for conservation projects requires a particular approach and specific skills. We are looking for sensitivity, an understanding of history, an understanding of the design concepts discussed in this book, a high level of visual literacy, and an ability to produce accurate and observant drawings. Great care is needed in the selection of the design team. Two suitable methods of finding these skills are to build up a record of successful schemes, either visited or featured in magazines, or to hold a competition. Sifted selection requires careful preparation of a short-list, such as the six considered for the restoration of Erich Mendelsohn's 1935 De La Warr Pavilion at Bexhill, based on their proven understanding of the Modern Movement ethic.[8]

Competitions are legally required in France for all government projects, and similar ideas are now being discussed in this country for projects over three million pounds.[9]

Competitions not only have the virtue of finding new young talent, but also of producing alternative schemes for consideration. This opportunity to choose from a range of options is not just a visual luxury but may well open the way to alternative and improved solutions. The competition must be fair and reasonable to all concerned. It is a touchy subject and it is advisable to set it up in conjunction with one of the professional bodies. There are basically two types of competition: the 'open competition' which is open to all to submit initial ideas, and the 'closed and limited design competition', wherein a selected group of practices are commissioned to produce a scheme for a fee.

The conventional form of building contract, wherein all the work is specified, costed, and constructed as one lump, is usually unsuitable for conservation projects. The factors are different, especially in the uncertainty as to what is going to be needed when the fabric is opened up. It is advisable to split the documents into separate contractual packages: for investigation, for opening up and removal of debris and unsalvageable fabric, for specialist renovation, and for new building work. It is particularly important to allow time to review the monument after the opening up to ascertain the actual state of the existing fabric. The apt adage of the carpenter's advice is 'think twice, you can only cut once'.

8.4 Quality

A recurring factor in good conservation projects is that thought and care extends right through the building, and that the details and the construction are carefully worked out to produce an inherent and consistent level of quality.

Quality is a key ingredient; this is easy to say but difficult to achieve. It requires a conscious effort, careful control, and a systematic approach.

Quality control is usually associated with the manufacturing process. It is easy to visualise the various checks of, for example, the production of a motor car, where every stage along the assembly line is separately monitored and checked. Architectural design and conservation practice are unfortunately not as predictable and repetitious as this, the process contains large chunks of mental rather than physical action. How then can we assert quality assurance alongside such a process? It is similarly possible to break down the conservation process into stages; divisions come to mind: identifying the need, selecting the team, deciding how the work should be carried out, selecting the most suitable form of contract, construction work off site, and construction work on site. Each of these can be subjected to a form of separate assessment, albeit, the type of control may be different for each.

Quality in a project does not simply mean throwing more money at the scheme,

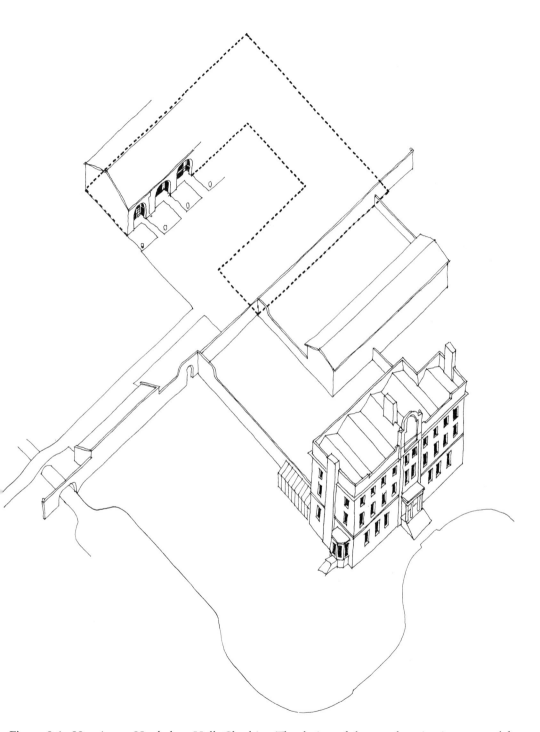

Figure 8.1. Housing at Hankelow Hall, Cheshire. The design of the new housing is generated from the footprint and images of a stable block. (scheme and drawing James Strike)

gold for bronze or teak for deal. Quality is in the attention to detail, care, the struggle for consistency, and an understanding that all decisions, large and small, have to portray the same architectural idea. The designer has to focus all of the various pragmatic requirements into a single piece of architecture.

8.5 Approach

To produce architecture at historic sites, which is both stimulating and sensitive, requires energy and enthusiasm. It is not for the faint-hearted or tired. There are so many obstacles to overcome; committees, design codes, town planning requirements, building regulations, fire precautions, safety requirements, let alone prejudice. One would assume that all of this control would prevent any change taking place, that control was designed to preserve the status quo. It should be remembered, however, that these controls were not set down to prevent good architecture, they are not a divisive trick to exclude modern schemes. Reading articles in the press, and HRH The Prince of Wales in *A Vision of Britain* (1989), may give this impression, but it is important to hold on to the belief that it is possible to work through these requirements to produce good architecture: hopefully the illustrations in this book demonstrate this. Colin Stanfield Smith, County Architect for Hampshire, 1973–91, was able to produce good architecture because he instilled into his team the idea that the end product was always more important than the administrative process.

Building Design magazine carried out a useful examination of the Prince of Wales's design codes. This report, 'Principles in perspective',[10] included an analysis by Roger FitzGerald to see how one of his own modernist projects stood up to the Prince's *Ten Principles*. The scheme was a swimming pool extension to a large private house overlooking the Thames in Oxfordshire (Fig. 8.2). FitzGerald's point-by-point comparison shows that the *Ten Principles* can equally be met by good modern architecture. *Hierarchy*, for example:

> The extension continues the internal organisation already established by the house: the main accommodation faces towards the river, whilst the service elements and circulation relate to the driveway.

And *Harmony*:

> The river elevation of the existing house was carefully analysed, and the existing elements were repeated or re-interpreted in the extension.

And *Decoration*:

> Any decoration was derived from necessity, the concrete circles are where access was required for post-tensioning and bolt connections.

The Prince of Wales's design codes may have been written to prevent 'the wanton destruction which has taken place in this country in the name of progress',[11] and to protect 'something rather special about Britain. . . . This character, which is so evident in the local architectural styles of the buildings you see in each

Figure 8.2. Swimming pool extension to house on the Thames, near Oxford. Architects Design Partnership. The detailing fulfils the Prince of Wales's *Ten Principles* of good design. (photographs Tony Weller)

Figure 8.3. Sackler Galleries, Royal Academy, Burlington House, Piccadilly, London. Foster Associates. (a) New glass lift and staircase inserted in the space between the two buildings: existing elevations restored by Julian Harrap. (photograph Dennis Gilbert)

148

Figure 8.3. (b) Junction of the new floor to the entablature of the existing wall; the glass edge panel provides a visual separation with the fabric. (photograph Martin Charles)

county';[12] but these attributes can equally be achieved through architecture which is of our time, which is modern and yet observant and sensitive.

The artist Ben Johnson is able to use historical references of buildings to achieve a truly twentieth-century image. His *Adam and Eve and All their Children*, for example, is historical, formal, symmetrical, yet modern. He is able to edit and synthesise the subject matter to produce the essence of the idea. The painting portrays the essence of history without the totality of the historical period (see section 3.8, 'Translation of ideas into architecture').[13]

There is no doubt that the debate has increased the general awareness about architecture (see section 2.2, 'Present attitudes'). This has led to a welcome debate about modern schemes carried out around the world, and out of this has emerged an appreciation of good modern architecture built at historic sites. It is pleasing that Norman Foster's work at Burlington House, Piccadilly, London, has received so much praise (Fig. 8.3). This, a carefully edited and well-crafted insertion to form the Sackler Galleries into the Royal Academy, is clear in the visual separation of what is new and what is historic. The glass lift and the glass staircase rise up through the void between the two buildings that form the Royal Academy. The new construction comes up to, but appears not to touch, the renovated historic elevations.[14] Its refinement is like the best of Elisabeth Lutyens's music which, described in her biography by Merion and Susie Harries, has similar qualities: 'music of aching purity – works like her Wittgenstein motet, and the Chamber Concerto 1 . . . brave, serious and unparochial'.[15] Foster's detailing and spatial relationship between the new and the old has that same edited and refined economy. This project is chosen as a suitably optimistic conclusion to this book.

This book set out to identify design concepts about architecture at historic sites. Hopefully, these concepts will be useful at the drawing board, but above all, they need to stimulate and inform. We need to encourage debate, and we particularly need to encourage informed debate about design concepts. The play *The Dwarfs*, by Harold Pinter, includes some absurd but incisive excursions into criticism. 'Len' observes of academic critics that, 'when they read a poem, they never open the door and go in. They bend down and squint through a keyhole.'[16]

Debate about modern architecture at historic sites is sometimes similar, it is often full of data and description but lacking in reasoned evaluation. Awareness of the design criteria involved is essential, and a knowledge of successful schemes broadens this awareness.

There is no need to be too systematic or moribund by analysis. The singer Josephine Barstow was willing to fall back on her well-trained and informed intuition to overcome her struggle with the role of Shostakovich's Lady Macbeth of Mtsensk:

> I just couldn't understand why she kept going round murdering people. Then I latched on to something in her last aria. She says, 'In the forest there's a black lake'. I decided that the lake was inside her.[17]

Renzo Piano describes the personal effort needed to understand the historical significance in what we design:

> When projects are of a highly complex nature, they need to be assimilated slowly: knowledge has to be stored up and you must know how to wait in silence, perhaps wandering around the site. During this period of silence something is happening: the historical and climatic aspects, which have conditioned the surroundings through the centuries, are absorbed and linked together.[18]

I hope that this book will help clients and designers to reach the full potential of their schemes.

Notes and references

1 Introduction

1 *Buildings at Risk, a Sample Survey*, London, English Heritage, 1992.
2 John and Nicola Ashurst, *Practical Building Conservation*, Aldershot, Gower Technical Press, 1988, vol. 1, p. 91.
3 Formerly Director of the International Centre for the Study of the Preservation and Restoration of Cultural Property (ICROM), Rome.
4 The basic principles of conservation were first tackled in Athens in 1931. This gathering of people contributed to the setting up of ICOMOS.
5 From the Introduction to the ICOMOS Charter of 1966.
6 A co-founder, and Vice-Chairman, of SAVE Britain's Heritage. Also Secretary of SPAB (the Society for the Protection of Ancient Buildings).
7 Secretary to the Royal Fine Arts Commission.
8 Umberto Eco, *Art and Beauty in the Middle Ages*, trans. M. Bredin, New Haven, Yale University Press, 1986, p. 12.

2 The field of study

1 Painted between 1892 and 1894. Ten canvases exhibited at the Royal Academy, London, in 1990. See Joachim Pissarro, *Monet's Cathedral*, London, Pavilion, 1990.
2 See Bryan Magee, *The Great Philosophers*, London, BBC Books, 1987, p. 195. See also Demetri Porphyrios, *Architectural History*, Architectural Design Profile, 1981, p. 96.
3 See Bryan Magee, op. cit., p. 192.
4 Built c.200AD. Over 3 kilometres in length and 6 metres in height. Built of Kentish ragstone facing with rubble infill and regular courses of flat brick.

5 Excavations around Richmond Green are beginning to disclose the extent of the buildings.
6 Particularly from the west range refectory which was remodelled into a terrace of houses.
7 See John Harvey, *The Mediaeval Architect*, London, Wayland, 1972, p. 82.
8 1457–99.
9 See David Watkin, *The Rise of Architectural History*, London, Architectural Press, 1980, p. 49.
10 Peter Davey, 'Without pastiche', in *Architectural Review*, December 1990.
11 Harris, Orgel, and Strong, *The King's Arcadia*, London, Arts Council, 1973, p. 142.
12 James Pope-Hennessy, *The Houses of Parliament*, London, Batsford, 1953, p. 20.
13 Fellow of Peterhouse College, and University of Cambridge Lecturer in History and Art.
14 Watkin, op. cit., p. 1.
15 Jane Fawcett (ed.) *The Future of the Past*, London, Thames & Hudson, 1976, p. 14.
16 Adrian Forty, 'The lure of the picturesque', in *Architecture Today*, September 1990, p. 44.
17 Christopher Hussey, *The Picturesque, Studies in a Point of View*, London, Frank Cass, 1927, p. 12.
18 M. W. Thompson, *Ruins, their Preservation and Display*, London, Colonnade Books/British Museum Publications, 1981, p. 14.
19 Glyn Coppack, *Abbeys and Priories*, London, Batsford, 1990, p. 18.
20 Quoted in Christopher Hussey, op. cit., p. 194. First published William Gilpin, *Observations on the River Wye, and Several Parts of South Wales, Relative Chiefly to Picturesque Beauty; Made in the Summer of the Year 1770*, London, R. Blamire, 1782, p. 32.
21 Mordaunt Crook, 'Strawberry Hill revisited', from *Country Life*, June 7–14–21, 1973.

22 See Muriel Spark, *Mary Shelley*, London, Constable, 1988.

23 Begun in 1833 under J. H. Newman and John Keble.

24 *Ecclesiologist* was the journal of the Cambridge Camden Movement. The name is used here in a general sense to include those Victorian architects whose work was influenced by High Church and obedience to past styles (e.g. Butterworth and Ruskin).

25 Gerald Cobb, *The English Cathedrals, the Forgotten Centuries*, London, Thames & Hudson, 1980, p. 14.

26 Jane Fawcett, op. cit., p. 77; B. Ferry, *Recollections of a Welby Pugin*, London, 1861, pp. 80–1.

27 See Richard Jenkins, *Dignity and Decadence*, San Francisco, HarperCollins, 1991, which deals with the nineteenth-century obsession for a classical inheritance.

28 Henry Cleere (ed.) *Archaeological Heritage Management*, London, Unwin Hyman, 1989, p. 1.

29 Together with women's suffrage, which began in 1866, leading to equal voting rights in 1928 (1920 in the USA).

30 See James Strike, *Construction into Design*, Oxford, Butterworth, 1991.

31 Ibid., p. 152.

32 Ibid., p. 155.

33 Döllgast had been teaching at Technische Hochschule since 1929.

34 Catalogue produced by *Architecture Today* for the exhibition of Döllgast's work, held at the Architectural Foundation, London, October 1991.

35 See Richard Murphy, *Carlo Scarpa and the Castelvecchio*, Oxford, Butterworth, 1990.

36 Speech for presentation of the Annual Report 1991.

37 1948–51, Robert Matthew and Leslie Martin. River front remodelled, Hubert Bennett, 1962.

38 1954, Adie Button and Partners.

39 *Evening Standard*, 15 July 1991.

40 Matthew D'Ancona, in *The Times*, 29 January 1992.

41 *RSA Journal*, August 1989, p. 577.

42 Martin Pawley, lecture, Conservation Conference, Dartington Hall, May 1991.

43 Based on his Reith lectures, 1955.

44 Kenneth Powell, 'A prophet without honour', in the *Daily Telegraph*, 9 November 1991. See also Sir James Stirling, obituary, *The Times*, 27 June 1992.

45 *Oxford English Dictionary* definition.

46 David Lowenthal, *The Past is a Foreign Country*, Cambridge, Cambridge University Press, 1985, paraphrased from p. 52.

47 George Steiner, 'Where burning Sappho loved and sung', review of Jenkyns, *Victorians and Ancient Greece*, in *New Yorker*, 9 February 1981, p. 115.

48 Archaeologist and Inspector for English Heritage.

49 Gill Chitty, 'A prospect of ruins', in ASCHB (Association for Studies in the Conservation of Historic Buildings) *Transactions*, vol. 12, 1987, p. 43.

50 R. W. Brunskill, *Vernacular Architecture*, London, Faber & Faber, 1971, pp. 194–7.

51 National Heritage Act 1983, Section 33.(1)(b).

52 Ibid., part (c).

53 Charles Knevitt, in *The Times*, 14 November 1990.

3 Connections by association

1 See M. D. Vernon, *The Psychology of Perception*, Harmondsworth, Pelican, 1962.

2 Adrian Forty, 'The trouble with common sense', in *Building Design*, 13 October 1989.

3 See Burnley Borough Council, *The Mill Chimney Report*, 1980.

4 Joseph Connelly, review of Peter Adam, *The Arts of the Third Reich* (published by Thames & Hudson in 1991), in *The Times*, 27 April 1992.

5 Warship Class 50 locomotives.

6 *Architectural Review*, January 1992.

7 Ibid., p. 19.

8 See Marcel Proust, *A la Recherche du temps perdu* (1922–31).

9 See James Strike, *Construction into Design*, Oxford, Butterworth, 1991.

10 Martin Wainwright, 'Town makes mockery of plastic ivy', in the *Guardian*, 13 August 1991.

11 Eco turned to semiotics in the early 1960s in search of an interdisciplinary understanding of art. He was a founder member of the avant-garde Group 63.

12 Martin Pawley, 'Ancient stones in glass houses', in the *Guardian*, 24 April 1989.

13 The work of Chillida was exhibited at the Hayward Gallery, London, September–November 1990.

14 Charlotte Barry, 'Swimming against the tide', in the *Observer* Magazine, 16 December 1990.

15 Italo Calvino, *Invisible Cities*, London, Picador, 1972, p. 17.

16 Ibid., p. 39.

17 Ibid., p. 16.

18 The work of Mena Hill was first exhibited at the

Duncan Campbell Fine Art Gallery, London, December 1990. See *Architectural Journal*, 28 November 1990.

19 Nessim J. Dawood, 'Reading a poem', in *The Times*, 18 January 1992.

20 Shakespeare, *Antony and Cleopatra*, act 4, scene 10.

21 Caroline Moorehead, 'The Eco effect', in *The Independent Magazine*, p. 53.

22 John Summerson, *The Classical Language of Architecture*, London, Thames & Hudson, 1963, p. 120.

23 Caroline Moorehead, op. cit.

24 World première, 18 May 1990, Coliseum, London.

25 Paul Driver in programme notes.

26 Nicolette Jones's report in *The Times*, 12 February 1989.

27 Ibid.

28 Ibid.

29 Craig Dykers and Cordula Mohr, 'Seat of learning', in *World Architecture* no. 10, 1991, p. 58.

30 E. H. Gombrich, *Art and Illusion*, London, Phaidon Press, 1960, p. 7.

4 Response to location

1 Dr Peled of the Technion-Israel Institute of Technology, including development of the *Location Task Technique*, a tool to enable users and designers to 'express their latent images of the spatial organisation of a place'.

2 Steen Eiler Rasmussen, *Experiencing Architecture*, Cambridge, Mass., MIT Press, 1959, p. 38.

3 Architectural Design Profile, *Cross Currents of American Architecture*, London, 1985, p. 45.

4 Dan Cruickshank, 'Oxford blues', in *Architectural Journal*, 3 April 1991.

5 R. E. Wycherley, *How the Greeks Built Cities*, London, W. W. Norton, 1962, Chapters I and II.

6 Sherban Cantacuzino, lecture to the Association of Conservation Officers, The Pythagoras Building, Cambridge, 1989.

7 Lawrence Gowing, *Matisse*, London, Thames & Hudson, 1979, Chapter 9.

8 Kevin Lynch, *What Time is this Place?*, Cambridge, Mass., MIT Press, 1972, p. 57.

9 Paper to the Department of Architecture, University of California, Berkeley, 'The teaching of preservation in the design studio: the relationship between theory and practice'.

10 David Keys, article in *The Independent*, 22 July 1991.

11 W. H. Hudson, *The Shepherd's Life*, London, Bodley Head, 1910, p. 15.

12 David Lowenthal, *The Past is a Foreign Country*, Cambridge, Cambridge University Press, 1985, p. 53.

13 Frank Barrett, 'Bath's beauty ruined by the architects', in *The Independent*, 13 December 1989.

14 John and Jane Penoyre, *Houses in the Landscape, a Regional Study of Vernacular Building Styles in England and Wales*, London, Faber & Faber, 1978.

15 Oliver Boissière, *Jean Nouvel*, Zurich, Artemis, 1992, Hôtel Saint-James, Bordeaux-Bouliac, p. 110, and Institut du Monde Arabe, p. 86.

16 Common Ground Organisation, *Local Distinctiveness*, pamphlet, 1990.

5 At the monument

1 Evelyn Waugh, *Brideshead Revisited*, Harmondsworth, Penguin, 1945, p. 44.

2 Geordie Greig, 'All change for the Wright stuff', in *The Sunday Times*, 28 June 1992.

3 Evolved from Peter Tonkin's competition-winning scheme. See Rory Spence, criticism in *Architecture Review*, April 1988, p. 26.

4 Ibid.

5 Thom Gorst, 'Frozen music: transforming the Catalan heritage', in *Architecture Today*, July 1990, p. 36.

6 Tim Benton, *Peter Behrens and the AEG Company*, Video, Open University Course, History of Architecture and Design 1890–1939.

7 Colin Rowe, 'Literal and phenomena transparency', in C. Rowe, *The Mathematics of the Ideal Villa*, Cambridge, Mass., MIT Press, 1976.

8 e.g. Georges Braque's painting *Flute Duet*, 1911.

9 Both examples taken from David Highfield, *The Construction of New Buildings behind Historic Facades*, London, Chapman & Hall, 1991.

10 Rowan More, 'It wasn't even good enough the first time round', in *The Independent*, 1 May 1991.

11 Richard Cork, criticism of Anish Kapoor's work, in *The Times*, 8 November 1991.

12 'Making places', February 1992.

13 See Richard Murphy, *Carlo Scarpa and the Castelvecchio*, Oxford, Butterworth, 1990.

14 Jonas Glemža and Romanas Jaloveckas, 'The renewal and restoration of part of the old town of Vilnius', in *Monumentum*, March 1984, p. 84.

15 David Pearce, *Conservation Today*, p. 180.

16 Sherban Cantacuzino, *Re-Architecture, Old*

Buildings/New Uses, London, Thames & Hudson, 1989, p. 31.
17 Formerly the Bethlem Royal Hospital, James Lewis, 1815. (Dome added by Sydney Smirke, 1845).
18 Article in *Architectural Review*, January 1991, p. 59.
19 Article in *Architecture Today*, September 1990, p. 28.
20 Based on an idea by Richard Negri.
21 John Matson, *Dear Osborne*, London, Hamish Hamilton, 1978, p. 35.
22 Bayan Northcott, 'The sound of silence', in *The Independent*, 21 December 1990.
23 These buildings were the subject of the controversy about style as recorded in Cinza Maria Sicca, *Committed to Classicism: the Building of Downing College, Cambridge*, Cambridge, Downing College, 1987.

6 Connections by assimilation

1 A. Sperling and K. Martin, *Psychology*, Oxford, Heinemann, 1982, p. 40.
2 Jonathan Glancey, 'Hi-tech rewrites of yesterday', in *The Independent*, 29 January 1992.
3 See Martin Meade, 'Iron in the soul', in *Architectural Review*, July 1988, p. 57.
4 Johannes Exner, 'Koldinghaus: the conversion of an old royal Danish castle', in *Monumentum*, December 1984, p. 285.
5 David Dunster (ed.) 'Venturi and Rauch', in *Architectural Monographs 1*, London, Academy Editions, 1978, p. 80.
6 Gavin Stamp (ed.), 'Crystal nightmares', in *The Independent*, 22 October 1988.
7 *Architectural Review*, September 1991, p. 9.
8 Kate Heron, 'Into the past', in *Architectural Review*, December 1991, p. 62.
9 Paul Wilkinson, 'Storm clouds gather over plan to annex Brontë heritage', in *The Times*, 6 June 1992.
10 Simon Jenkins, 'Triumph for modern master', in *The Times*, 4 May 1991.
11 Ada Louise Huxtable, 'Why the critics got it wrong', in the *Daily Telegraph*, 25 July 1991.
12 'Free-style classicism', in *Architectural Design*, no. 52, 1982.
13 Bayan Northcott, 'Memories regained', in *The Independent*, 4 May 1991.
14 At the School of Architecture, Kingston University.
15 The subject of his book of the same title. See, for example, the residence in Chestnut Hill, Pa., p. 118.

16 John Summerson, *The Classical Language of Architecture*, London, Thames & Hudson, 1963, Fig. 48.
17 Vitruvius (Roman architect working in the reign of Emperor Augustus) *The Ten Books of Architecture*, which contained constant reference to Greek ancestry. Alberti, 1404–72, *De Re Aedificatoria*, ten books based on Vitruvius. Andrea Palladio, 1508–80, *Quattro Libri dell' Architectura*, which includes applications of the orders through examples of both antiquity and his own works. Claude Perrault, 1613–88, for the great tradition of French Renaissance thought. William Chambers, 1723–96, *A Treatise on Civil Architecture*.
18 John Summerson, op. cit., Chapter 2.
19 See 'Free-style architecture', in *Architectural Design*, no. 52, 1982.
20 Francis Golding, *Conservation Bulletin*, October 1989, p. 15.

7 Presence or anonymity

1 The John Woods, father and son, mid-eighteenth century.
2 Rock Townsend, *Royal Leamington Spa*, London, Warwick District Council/English Heritage, 1990.
3 Began in the 1760s.
4 27 June 1850.
5 Hall burned down in 1833.
6 Dr and Mrs Cooper.
7 Tanya Harrod, 'In the company of Soane and after', in *The Independent*, 30 September 1990.
8 Murray Frasser, 'Vanishing act', in *Architectural Journal*, 18 July 1990.
9 Callum Murray, 'Now you see it, now you don't', in *The Times*, 21 August 1990; a review of Dewar, *The Art of Deception in Warfare*, Newton Abbot, Devon, David & Charles, 1989.
10 Jonathan Alexander and Paul Binski, *Age of Chivalry*, London, Royal Academy of Arts/Weidenfeld & Nicolson, 1987, Ch. XIV.
11 John Ruskin, 'The lamp of memory' section II in *The Seven Lamps of Architecture*, London, 1849.
12 *RIBA Journal*, August 1991.
13 Dinah Casson lecture at the conference 'Intervention: the conservation dilemma', Royal Institute of British Architects and Plymouth School of Architecture, Dartington Hall, Totnes, Devon, May 1991.
14 Jeff West, Regional Director for English Heritage Properties, Midlands, Peer group review, 21 October 1991.

155

15 Richard Boston, 'The face of the Angel', in the *Guardian*, 17 June 1991.
16 Roger White lecture at the conference 'Intervention: the conservation dilemma', Royal Institute of British Architects and Plymouth School of Architecture, Dartington Hall, Totnes, May 1991.
17 Gill Chitty, 'A prospect of ruins', in ASCHB (Association for Studies in Conservation of Historic Buildings) *Transactions*, vol. 12, 1987, p. 43.
18 Matthew Coomber, 'Keeping up appearances', in *Building*, 26 June 1992.
19 Anthony Emery, *Commission Paper 87/36*, London, English Heritage, March 1987.
20 Graham Fairclough, *New Uses for Old Ruins, Policy Framework for Unroofed Structures*, London, English Heritage, 1991.
21 Glyn Coppack, *Abbeys and Priories*, London, Batsford/English Heritage, 1990.
22 Constructed 1812–14.
23 For example, the United Presbyterian Church, Caledonia Road, Glasgow, 1856.
24 Umberto Eco, *The Open Work*, Cambridge, Mass., Hutchinson Radius, 1989, p. 181.
25 Bryan Magee, *The Great Philosophers*, London, BBC Books, 1987, p. 173.
26 For example, the interior of Portsmouth Town Hall

8 The way forward

1 See H. F. Cleere, *Archaeological Heritage Management in the Modern World*, London, Unwin Hyman, 1989.
2 Paper to the Department of Architecture, University of California, Berkeley, 'The teaching of preservation in the design studio: the relationship between theory and practice'.
3 Ibid., p. 13.
4 Ibid., p. 15.
5 Ralph Knott, 1903–22.
6 Letters in *The Times* from Sir Mcleod, 30 March 1992, and Sir Hugh Casson, 11 April 1992. And Gavin Stamp, 'Time to restore London's pride' in *The Independent*, 8 November 1989.
7 Stephen Games's review of Mary Midgley, *Wisdom, Information and Wonder*, in the *Guardian*, 31 March 1989.
8 *Building Design*, 17 May 1991.
9 'Decade of design', in *The Times*, 24 July 1991.
10 *Building Design*, 24 November 1989.
11 HRH The Prince of Wales, *Vision of Britain*, New York, Doubleday, 1989, p. 7.
12 Ibid., p. 17.
13 Rowan More, 'Portrait of the artist as a builder of paintings', in *The Independent*, 3 October 1990.
14 Existing elevations renovated by Julian Harrap.
15 Book review of Merion and Susie Harries, 'Elisabeth Lutyens', in *The Sunday Times*, 5 November 1989.
16 Jonathan Coe review of the play *The Dwarfs* by Harold Pinter, in the *Guardian*, 27 September 1990.
17 Hilary Finch, 'Beware the harridan who may tear your voice apart', in *The Times*, 11 October 1990.
18 *Domus*, November 1987.

Bibliography

Details of magazine features and press articles are given within the main text or credited in the Notes and References.

Alexander, Christopher (1964) *Notes on the Synthesis of Form*, Cambridge, Mass.: Harvard University Press.

Alexander, Jonathan and Binski, Paul (eds) (1987) *Age of Chivalry, Art in Plantagenet England 1200–1400*, London: Royal Academy of Arts/Weidenfeld & Nicolson.

Ashurst, John and Ashurst, Nicola (1988) *Practical Building Conservation, English Heritage Technical Handbook, Volumes 1 to 5*, Aldershot: Gower Technical Press.

Baker, Geoffrey (1989) *Design Strategies in Architecture, An Approach to the Analysis of Form*, London: Chapman & Hall.

Boissière, Oliver (trans. Ronald Corlette-Theuil) (1992) *Jean Nouvel*, Zurich: Studio Paperback, Artemis.

Bonta, J.P. (1979) *Architecture and its Interpretation*, London: Lund Humphries.

Brunskill, R.W. (1971) *Vernacular Architecture*, London: Faber & Faber.

Burton, Neil (1989) *English Heritage from the Air*, London: Sidgwick & Jackson.

Calvino, Italo (1972) *Invisible Cities*, London: Picador.

Cantacuzino, Sherban (1989) *Re-Architecture, Old Buildings/New Uses*, London: Thames & Hudson.

Chitham, Robert (1985) *The Classical Orders of Architecture*, London: Architectural Press.

Cleere, H.F. (ed.) (1989) *Archaeological Heritage Management in the Modern World*, London: Unwin Hyman.

Cobb, Gerald (1980) *The English Cathedrals, the Forgotten Centuries*, London: Thames & Hudson.

Colegate, Isabel (1980) *The Shooting Party*, Harmondsworth: Penguin.

Colquhoun, Alan (1981) *Essays in Architectural Criticism – Modern Architecture and Historical Change*, Cambridge, Mass.: MIT Press.

Coppack, Glyn (1990) *Abbeys and Priories*, London: Batsford/English Heritage.

Dal Co, Francesco (1987) *Mario Botta 1960–1985*, London: Electa/Architectural Press.

D'Arcy Thompson (1942) *Growth and Form*, Cambridge: Cambridge University Press.

Dewar, Michael (1989) *The Art of Deception in Warfare*, Newton Abbot, David & Charles.

Dormer, Peter (1990) *The Meaning of Modern Design: Towards the Twenty-First Century*, London: Thames & Hudson.

Eco, Umberto (trans. Hugh Bredin) (1986) *Art and Beauty in the Middle Ages*, New Haven: Yale University Press.

Eco, Umberto (trans. Anna Cancogni) (1989) *The Open Work*, Cambridge, Mass.: Hutchinson Radius/Harvard University.

Fawcett, Jane (ed.) (1976) *The Future of the Past, Attitudes to Conservation 1147–1974*, London: Thames & Hudson.

Feilden, Bernard (1982) *Conservation of Historic Buildings*, Oxford: Butterworth.

Ferrey, B. (1861) *Recollections of a Welby Pugin*, London.

Freeman, Andrew (1921) *English Organ-Cases*, London: Mate & Son.

Gilpin, William (1782) *Observations on the River Wye, and Several Parts of South Wales, Relative Chiefly to Picturesque Beauty; Made in the Summer of the Year 1770*, London: R. Blamire.

Gombrich, E.H. (1960) *Art and Illusion*, London: Phaidon Press

Gowing, Lawrence (1979) *Matisse*, London: Thames & Hudson.

Grass, Günter (trans. Ralph Manheim) (1959) *The Tin Drum*, London: Picador.

Hardy, Thomas (1978) *The Mayor of Casterbridge* (1st edition 1886), London: Pan Macmillan.

Harries, Meirion and Susie (1989) *A Pilgrim Soul: The Life and Works of Elizabeth Lutyens*, London: Faber.

Harris, John, Orgel, Stephen, and Strong, Roy (1973) *The King's Arcadia: Inigo Jones and the Stuart Court*, London: Arts Council of Great Britain.

Harvey, John (1972) *The Mediaeval Architect*, London: Wayland.

Hewison, Robert (1987) *The Heritage Industry – Britain in a Climate of Decline*, London: Methuen.

Highfield, David (1991) *The Construction of New Buildings behind Historic Facades*, London: E. and F.N. Spon (Chapman & Hall).

Hillier, Bill and Hudson, Julienne (1984) *The Social Logic of Space*, Cambridge: Cambridge University Press.

Hough, Michael (1990) *Out of Place, Restoring Regional Landscapes*, New Haven: Yale University Press.

HRH, The Prince of Wales (1989) *A Vision of Britain: A Personal View*, New York: Doubleday.

Hudson, W. H. (1910) *The Shepherd's Life*, London: Bodley Head.

Hussey, Christopher (1927) *The Picturesque, Studies in a Point of View*, London: Frank Cass.

Jencks, Charles (1990) *The New Moderns*, London: Academy Editions.

Jenkins, Richard (1991) *Dignity and Decadence*, San Francisco: HarperCollins.

Kamen, Ruth (1981) *British and Irish Architectural History: A Bibliography and Guide to Sources of Information*, London: Architectural Press.

Krier, Rob (1979) *Urban Space*, London: Academy Editions.

Lawson, Bryan (1980) *How Designers Think, The Design Process Demystifed*, Oxford: Butterworth.

Lowenthal, David (1985) *The Past is a Foreign Country*, Cambridge: Cambridge University Press.

Lynch, Kevin (1972) *What Time is this Place?*, Cambridge, Mass.: MIT Press.

Macaulay, James (1975) *The Gothic Revival 1745–1845*, Glasgow: Blackie.

Macaulay, Rose (1953) *The Pleasures of Ruins*, New York: Walker.

Magee, Bryan (1987) *The Great Philosophers*, London: BBC Books.

March, Lionel and Steadman, Philip (1971) *The Geometry of the Environment*, London: RIBA Publications.

Matson, John (1978) *Dear Osborne*, London: Hamish Hamilton.

Midgley, Mary (1989) *Wisdom, Information and Wonder*, London: Routledge.

Moughtin, Cliff (1992) *Urban Design, Street and Square*, Oxford: Butterworth.

München Technische Universität, Bund Deutscher Architekten (1987) *Hans Döllgast 1891–1974*, Munich: George Callwey.

Murphy, Richard (1990) *Carlo Scarpa and the Castelvecchio*, Oxford: Butterworth.

Murray, Peter (1969) *The Architecture of the Italian Renaissance*, London: Thames & Hudson.

Norberg-Schulz, Christian (1979) *Genius Loci, Towards a Phenomenology of Architecture*, New York: Rizzoli.

Pearce, David (1989) *Conservation Today*, London: Routledge.

Penoyre, John and Jane (1978) *Houses in the Landscape, A Regional Study of Vernacular Building Style in England and Wales*, London: Faber & Faber.

Pevsner, Nikolaus (1956) *The Englishness of English Art*, Harmondsworth: Peregrine.

Pissarro, Joachim (1990) *Monet's Cathedral*, London: Pavilion.

Polano, Sergio (1988) *Hendrick Petrus Berlage*, Oxford: Butterworth.

Pope-Hennessy, James (1953) *The Houses of Parliament*, London: Batsford.

Powys, A.R. (1981) *Repair of Ancient Buildings*, London: SPAB.

Rasmussen, Steen Eiler (1959) *Experiencing Architecture*, Cambridge, Mass.: MIT Press.

RCHME (Royal Commission on the Historical Monuments of England) (1991) *County Hall, Survey of London Monograph 17*, London: Athlone Press.

Rowe, Colin (1976) *The Mathematics of the Ideal Villa*, Cambridge, Mass.: MIT Press.

Ruskin, John (1849) *The Seven Lamps of Architecture*, London: Smith Elder & Co.

Schmidt, Hartwig (1988) *Schutz Bauten*, Berlin: Architekture ferat des Deutschen Archälogischen Instituts/Stuttgart: Konrad Theiss Verlag GmbH.

Scruton, Roger (1979) *The Aesthetics of Architecture*, London: Methuen.

Shaffer, Peter (1988) *Lettice and Lovage*, Harmondsworth: Penguin Plays.

Sharp, Thomas (1946) *The Anatomy of the Village*, Harmondsworth: Penguin.

Sicca, Cinza Maria (1987) *Committed to Classicism: The Building of Downing College, Cambridge*, Cambridge: Downing College.

Spark, Muriel (1988) *Mary Shelley*, London: Constable.

Sperling, A. and Martin, K. (1982) *Psychology*, Oxford: Heinemann.

Stamp, Gavin (ed.) (1979) *Britain in the Thirties*, AD Profile No. 24.

Strike, James (1991) *Construction into Design, the Influence of New Methods of Construction on Architectural Design 1690–1990*, Oxford: Butterworth Architecture.

Summerson, John (1963) *The Classical Language of Architecture*, London: Thames & Hudson.

Thompson, M.W. (1981) *Ruins, their Preservation and Display*, London: Colonnade Books/British Museum Publications.

Townsend, Rock (1990) *Royal Leamington Spa, a Design Framework in an Historic Town*, London: Warwick District Council and English Heritage.

Tugnutt, Anthony and Robertson, Mark (1987) *Making Townscape. A Contextual Approach to Building in an Urban Setting*, London: Batsford.

Tzonis and Lefaivre (1986) *Classical Architecture, The Poetics of Order*, Cambridge Mass.: MIT Press.

Venturi, Robert, Scott-Brown, Denise, and Izenour, Stevens (1966) *Complexity and Contradiction in Architecture*, New York: The Museum of Modern Art.

Venturi, Robert, Scott-Brown, Denise, and Izenour, Stevens (1972) *Learning from Las Vegas*, Cambridge, Mass.: MIT Press.

Vernon, M.D. (1962) *The Psychology of Perception*, Harmondsworth: Pelican.

Watkin, David (1980) *The Rise in Architectural History*, London: Architectural Press.

Watkin, David (1982) *The English Vision: The Picturesque in Architecture, Landscape and Garden Design*, London: John Murray.

Waugh, Evelyn (1981) *Brideshead Revisited* (1st edn 1945), Harmondsworth: Penguin.

Web, Michael (1990) *The City Square*, London: Thames & Hudson.

Wycherley, R.E. (1962) *How the Greeks Built Cities*, London: W.W. Norton.

Index